TWENTY QUESTIONS ABOUT A UNIFIED THEORY OF INFORMATION

A Short Exploration into Information from a Complex Systems View

TWENTY QUESTIONS ABOUT A UNIFIED THEORY OF INFORMATION

A Short Exploration into Information from a Complex Systems View

---

Wolfgang Hofkirchner

EMERGENT™
PUBLICATIONS

The cover image is a detail of an artwork by Korean-born painter Young-Ja Zimmermann who has been living in Germany since 1970—Roter Planet (2006), Mischtechnik auf Leinwand, 60x80 cm). When combining different styles originating in European abstract art and East-Asian tradition as well as different materials, as in collage design, she reflects unity through diversity and "the utopian moment in each effort aiming at reconciling what is different" (http://www.koreanarts.de/).

Twenty Questions About a Unified Theory of Information:
A Short Exploration into Information from a Complex Systems View
Written by: Wolfgang Hofkirchner

Library of Congress Control Number:
    2010931756

ISBN: 978-0-9842164-7-5

Copyright © 2010
Emergent Publications,
3810 N. 188th Ave, Litchfield Park, AZ 85340, USA

Printed in the United States of America

I want to thank the Foundation for the Open University of Catalonia which subsidized my stay at the Internet Interdisciplinary Institute in Barcelona where I could find time to prepare this publication.

Thanks go to the Paris-Lodron University of Salzburg too which allowed me a leave of absence.

CONTENTS

TABLES AND FIGURES

PREFACE

This timely booklet will be released on the eve of the first-ever international conference 'Towards a New Science of Information', held in Beijing on 20–23 August, 2010.

This is a short introduction into what I and my co-workers, especially from my UTI Research Group in Vienna, have been used to calling 'Unified Theory of Information (UTI)'. UTI may thus be regarded as a specific proposal of what theoretical foundations of a new science of information could look like, and tries to connect complex systems thinking to systems philosophy and extend it to the field of information studies.

Since this approach was recognized by Rafael Capurro and Birger Hjørland (2003), as well as Luciano Floridi (2004), several refinements have been made to our framework. This booklet presents elaborations in a concise format which I hope makes it an easy read. The chapters might be read independently but there is a thread that connects them.

I owe special thanks to Kurt Richardson who made this publication possible in a very short time.

The text is based upon, and is a major revision of, another text I wrote in 2007/2008 and which was published under the Creative Commons License (2009). Three chapters underwent substantial change, figures were redrawn, one chapter was completely rewritten and a new chapter was added, while another one was omitted.

Many changes are owed to intensive discussions with Francisco Salto Alemany and José María Díaz Nafría during my stay at the University of León in the fall of 2009.

Wolfgang Hofkirchner
Barcelona, May 2010

Q1. A UNIFIED THEORY OF INFORMATION (UTI)— WHAT'S IT FOR?

A t first glance, it seems an intra-scientific issue of whether or not in the field of information there is an attempt to grasp the big picture and develop a shared theory by which the whole variety of different manifestations of information processes in society and in the world at all might be understood. As in everyday thinking where people strive to connect unconnected experiences and even reconcile irreconcilable experiences, in order to arrive at a coherent overall view, so science is heading for 'consilience'. This term attracted interest when Edward O. Wilson published his book of the same title (1998), and is a unity of knowledge that allows for better explanations and predictions. This is accomplished via the construction of new theories that include the findings of old theories as approximations and, at the same time, are able to explain and predict phenomena that were not covered by the old theories. Thus, in science, there is a tendency towards more overarching theories, more generalizing theories and more universal theories. Unified theories address the universal by unifying the multiplicity of as yet incoherent theories bound to particular levels. Unified theories belong to the intra-scientific progress towards the universal.

However, it is not just a case of pure scientific curiosity. If we take into account that science is not kept within an ivory tower but is a social undertaking that satisfies social demands, then it does not come as a surprise that, on the threshold of the 'Information Age', science is concerned with information and that there is a quest for a unified theory of information (UTI) (Hofkirchner, 1999).

The Information Age is the age of information societies into which industrialized societies are transforming, and which is visible by the spread of new information and communication technologies (ICTs), while the 'Industrial Age' is the age of industrial societies into which agricultural societies have been transforming worldwide. Each transformation is known as a 'revolution' and all revolutions together are said to form the evolution of civilization (see Figure 1).

On one hand, there is a lag of scientific development behind societal and technological development. Development in technology is not accompanied by an equally rapid growth in scientific insight, let alone foresight, into the impacts of technology on society.

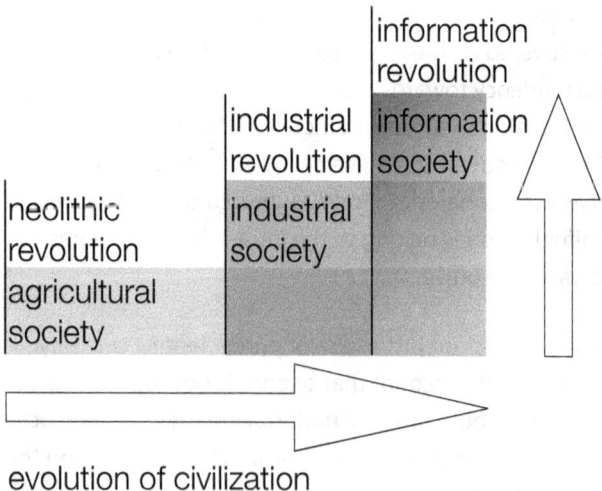

evolution of civilization

Figure 1 *From Industrial Societies to Information Societies*

Attempts to observe and understand the basic nature of this change still take second place. The public use of the term 'information society' has been reduced to denoting a society in which applications of modern ICT are spread widely in order to facilitate the handling of what is commonly called 'information'. A scientific understanding of this transformation has not had time to develop. There is not yet a proper 'science of the information society' nor a proper 'science of information'.

On the other hand, the state of the relationship between science and modern techno-social development regarding information can, for example, be compared to the state with which Karl Marx was confronted with regard to work. In his time work could become, and became, a matter of scientific interest, since work gained a new role in society and became more abstract in social life; that is, it was treated in society irrespective of its concrete characteristics. Marx called that a 'real-abstraction'; an abstraction that occurred in reality owing to the real treatment of work in the emerging capitalism which became the basis for the general concept of work in scientific thought. It was only then that the concept of work could be stretched back to former social life in the history of humanity, as well as other phenomena than industrial work which could be subsumed under the concept of work, albeit as different manifestations. Making use of this notion of real-abstraction we might assume that, nowadays, information has gained as decisive a role in society, in order to foster a new scientific concept and theorizing; that it has turned into a real-abstraction which is the rationale for devising a general idea as well. How work is regarded in human history, when seen from the perspective of industrial society, so, too, is information regarded in history when viewed from the perspective of information society.

What then has changed with information? Is it just the quantity of what can be conveyed by ICTs? Or is the quantity of information just the indication for a qualitative change taking place?

There has been a qualitative change in the role information can play for the development of society, and this change is unprecedented in the history of humanity. Information has become the bearer of survival, the key to our future. The information age is, fundamentally, the age of global challenges. The impressions made by the atomic bomb, industrial and agricultural catastrophes, hunger, suffering and death in the poor parts of the world, starting in the middle of the twentieth century but persistent in the new millennium, have raised consciousness of the destructive and fallible nature of the human technosphere, the fragile and finite nature of the human ecosphere, and the unsettled, unbalanced nature of the human sociosphere.

It is generally known that the existence of such global challenges can endanger today's societies all over the world. The global problems are global in a twofold sense: first, they concern humankind as a whole (as an object); second, they can only be solved by humankind as a whole (as a subject). The risk this crisis carries is that humankind may be wiped out. The chance it offers, however, is that humankind may be raised to another level of humanity.

It is disparities in the development of the relationships amongst humans, between humans and nature and between humans and technology, that create obstacles to keeping society as a whole on a stable, steady path of development. It is malfunctions in the sociosphere, ecosphere and technosphere that continue to aggravate the global challenges. And it is information that turns out the only remedy. It is information that is required to steer society. It is information that is required to reorganize humanity onto a higher level of organization. It is information that is required to alleviate and reduce the frictions (Heylighen, 2008) in the functioning of those systems that make up humanity: from the individual to different ethnic groups to nations to world society; from economy to politics to culture, from society to ecology to technology; from the social realm to the biotic realm to the physical realm.

In a word, the continued existence of humanity has shaped up as impossible without conscious and cautious intervention in the process of its own development. This intervention that is moving towards the reconnection of our disintegrating world—which is falling apart owing to processes of heterogenization, fragmentation and disintegration—is informational in nature, but as it extends from the human sphere to the living sphere to the material sphere, it necessitates a deep understanding of the information processes going on in the world we inhabit.

Knowledge as capacity to act means that today the capacity to act vis-à-vis global challenges means knowledge about how information guides the processes that put us at risk. Hence information is the *conditio sine qua non* for the further existence and development of humanity.

From this perspective, a UTI makes sense.

Q2. WHAT MAKES A UTI DISTINCT FROM 'NORMAL SCIENCE' INFORMATION STUDIES?

A UTI is part of a secular paradigm change towards complex thinking in the field of information studies. How does it differ from information studies in the 'normal science' mode?

Traditionally, there has been a distinction between applied sciences and basic sciences which, it is widely believed, is now becoming blurred. The image of an engineer employed in a private laboratory, taking orders from his employer contrasts sharply with the image of an academic satisfying his curiosity, who is said to be old-fashioned and outdated. It is true that scientists enjoy a freedom of research within certain financial, policy and other constraints. But this is rather owing to the fact that, from the last quarter of the previous century, research and development have been streamlined world-wide according to neoliberal economic policies of liberalization, privatization, and deregulation, rather than as a result of the general statement that science at any time is part of society and thus responsive, directly or indirectly, to historically developing societal needs. Otherwise one could not explain why in developed and thus rich countries many disciplines, in particular in the humanities, are stigmatized publicly as beautiful but useless and suffer cuts and suspensions. It is the short-sighted economic interest that has taken command in scientific affairs. Thus it makes still sense to distinguish between business-driven development of science and technology and *l'art pour l'art* activities.

Accordingly, information concepts might tend to either give some foundation for ICT applications or to be very detached from real-world problems.

Given the confines of economic profitability and competitiveness, the credo of technocracy runs as follows: 'realize everything that is feasible'. Thereby, it is presupposed falsely that everything feasible (again, it is taken for granted that it is economically reasonable) is also desirable and so a reflective, theoretical, deliberation of norms, values, morals is not needed or, at best, is replaced by *a posteriori*, empirical inquiries about the acceptance of technology by users. In fact, this detracts from taking into account problems that are more fundamental than those of rentability. The most striking historical example for an information concept in line with this tendency is the one developed in the context of a pure technological problem (though arising from military concerns) in the Bell Laboratories after World War II. It is still called 'Information Theory' and is a branch of mathematics and engineering inaugurated by Claude E. Shannon's paper *A Mathematical Theory of Communication* (1948) that dealt with the problem of keeping under control the signal-noise-ratio in communication transmission channels.

Information concepts devoid of considerations about their possibly far-reaching impact on society are often subjected to dominating economic, political and military interests. This may, in the end, also be true of conceptualizations that are intended to serve no purpose except keeping within the borders of the ivory tower. Though refusing subsumption under instrumental rationality they are produced under determinate historical circumstances which may make them, unwillingly, inhere certain values. Anything imaginable may be influenced by the state-of-the-art of already produced imagination. Complete refusal of applicability is thus not reasonable.

Concerning the opposition of applied science and basic science, Pasteur's Quadrant offers a solution. Donald Stokes (1997: 12) produced a 4 x 4 matrix with the 'Quest for fundamental Understanding' as one dimension and 'Consideration of Use' as another, with yes and no answers for each. While for Stokes Thomas Alva Edison is the role model for pure applied research and Niels Bohr the example of pure basic research, it is Louis Pasteur whom he deems paradigmatic of a new way of doing science: 'use-inspired basic research'.

A UTI underlying a new science of information certainly belongs to Pasteur's Quadrant and needs openness for being inspired by use when searching for a fundamental understanding of information. However, use must not be understood in a restricted economic, political, military or technological sense. What is needed is openness to taking into account the great challenges humanity is confronted with in the modern age and an according prioritization of values. The *raison d'être* of a UTI as core of a science of information is to provide society with a means of enhancing its problem-solving capacity vis-à-vis these challenges, to make it have a future, to make it 'futurable'.

A vision of the 'good society' must serve as point of departure. A good society, given the global challenges, can be defined as a society that:

- Is capable of making use of knowledge;
- Fights the dangers of breakdown owing to anthropogenic causes, and;
- Exists on a global scale.

In this sense, a UTI is normative. Technological applications should be questioned and the question is: Are they apt to serve the purpose of a good society? The process of design must start with identifying a societal problem and continue with the search for appropriate applications (not the other way round as is done under technocratic premises).

In this context, a UTI-inspired science of information implies a transgression from the scientists to the stakeholders and those affected by the results of research, and a transformation into a new science that is human-centred, democratic and participatory, like Helga Nowotny's 'Mode-2' science (Gibbons and Nowotny, 2002).

Q3. WHAT IS THE EXTENSION OF THE CONCEPT OF INFORMATION IN A UTI?

'Information' is the super-concept; a generic concept. It covers different manifestations of real-world information processes, regardless of the realm in which they appear.

It is clear that 'information' is related closely to a bunch of similar concepts. To choose one them and illuminate how it is linked to the others is rather arbitrary; it is more a terminological issue. What matters is the intention of the concept; that is, what it means and how the network of relations is conceived.

Here is an incomplete list of concepts that are related to the super-concept of 'information' and are, to a greater or lesser extent, comprised of it; that is, to different degrees, they overlap with 'information':

- Structure;
- Data;
- Signal;
- Message;
- Signification, meaning, sense;
- Sign;
- Sign process, semiosis;
- Psyche;
- Intelligence;
- Perception;
- Thought;

- Language;
- Knowledge;
- Consciousness, mind, and;
- Wisdom …

For practical reasons, it makes sense to make use of the following distinction, which I introduced earlier (Hofkirchner, 2002; Hofkirchner & Stockinger, 2003); the Triple-C Model.

We come across information in three areas of society:

- In the area of cognition, where the contents of consciousness are produced by individuals;
- In the area of communication, where common understanding is produced by interactions (individuals), and;
- In the area of cooperation, where sense embodied in societal structures is produced collectively by individuals who act in balanced ways.

The first and second areas are self-explanatory, with cognitive science and communication studies well-known fields of scientific activity. The third area is unconventional, as it contests a strong tradition in the humanities that qualifies society as composed of communications only. Niklas Luhmann propounds this tradition (1997). Introducing cooperation does justice to the 'social facts' Emile Durkheim considered the proper object of sociology; to the 'social relationships' Karl Marx distinguished from 'social behavior'; to the 'structure' that was focused on by the structuralist school after Marx; to the 'synergy effects' that today can be investigated by science-of-complexity methods. That is, this concept does justice to the phenomenon that there is more to society than only communication on the level of individuals' interaction and that this whole, which is more than the sum of communications/interactions, is an information process too, albeit on the level of a social group.

So we can say that a UTI comprises human cognition, communication and cooperation processes. All three are, in a way, normative: cognition positions the individual vis-à-vis the societal, social and non-human environment; communication aims to find a state of mutual understanding between individuals on whatever matter it may be; and cooperation has a goal, that of individual organization that allows for a mutually beneficial common outcome. As a consequence, cognitive science, communication studies, cultural studies, social science, humanities, arts and the like are sciences that enquire into human information processes.

But 'information' is not a concept that applies to humans only. A UTI has to apply it to the precursors of human information processes as well. Cognition is not only a process on the human level, you will find it within other organisms as well. The same holds for communication, as well as cooperation. Furthermore, it depends on the intension of the 'information' concept, as to whether or not also precursors of organismic cognitive, communicative and cooperative information processes can be identified in the pre-biotic world.

Q4. WHAT ARE THE THEORIES/ CONCEPTS OF INFORMATION THAT A UTI ATTEMPTS TO UNIFY?

There are several possible classifications for this. The oldest way to classify information concepts/theories, with a long grounding in philosophy, is to enquire into the essence of information, the nature of information and the substance out of which it is made. This is a question which is answered in relation to the essence, nature and substance of matter.

The first answer is that information is of the same substance as matter; this substance is conceived as something material and so information is material. This answer is material(istic) monism: everything is like matter and so is information. This is called materialism.

Or this substance is said to be immaterial and then information is immaterial. This answer is immaterial (ideal, idealistic, ideational, informational) monism, idealism: also matter is like the mind (information). Varieties are Platonism and Radical Constructivism.

Another answer is that matter and information do not share substance: they are essentially different in nature. Matter is material and information is not: this is the dualistic answer. Here another question arises: Are these two substances inert, and do not react to each other, or do they interact and, if so, how then can one side of the duality affect the other? How is it possible that matter influences the mind (information)? How is it possible for the mind (information) to be efficacious on matter? Suffice to say, the Cartesian tradition and, more recently, John

Eccles and Karl Raimund Popper (1977) tried to give an answer .

Since this classification is a philosophical one, it belongs to the most abstract classification.

Broken down from philosophy to an account of the disciplines, there is the gap between (natural) science and social and human science that has to be considered in approaching information. For example, a gap between natural science and engineering (including formal sciences) on the one hand and the arts and humanities (including social sciences) on the other hand, that dates back to the 17th century and to philosophers such as René Descartes. The gap between the two branches of science reached its peak in the late 19th century with the works of the Neo-Kantian philosophers, scientists and literary intellectuals such as Wilhelm Windelband and Heinrich Rickert. Windelband (1894), for example, introduced the disjunction between 'nomothetic' (meaning: the law) and 'ideographic' (meaning: the event), which remain alongside one another as the final, incommensurable forms of our notions about the world. Today this division is known as 'C. P. Snow's dilemma' which Snow bemoaned in 1959 and 1963 (1998).

The science and technology side of this argument is characterized by a technologically bound rationality which rests upon the obsolete equation of social and scientific-technological progress. The second is characterized by a humanistic rationality which is ignorant of science and technology. So are the categories of information concepts.

The first approach is inclined to be reductionistic in its method. It reduces different qualities of the phenomena under investigation to one and the same quality which is the most simple as a rule. It can be said that this approach looks upon information as something that can be received, stored, processed, exchanged, used and so on, like a thing. It is the 'hard' science standpoint and holds also for cognition, communication and cooperation processes in society, as well as for natural domains.

The second approach is biased, insofar as it takes its point of departure from the stance of humanities. Methodologically, there are two possibilities. Either it projects one particular quality in question which, as a rule, is the most complex one, onto phenomena that do not possess this quality, and pretends to be able to discover them there. Properties of information in non-human domains are usually extrapolated from properties of information in the human domain (anthropo(socio) morphism). Beyond that, properties of cognition may be extrapolated from those of communication, and those of communication, in turn, from those of cooperation within the human domain itself.

Or the attempt at a subsuming, though unifying, solution is given up and it is argued in favour of a lack of comparability of the given phenomena in nature and society. In this dichotomizing view, information is ascribed exclusively to the human domain. Beyond that, it may be ascribed exclusively to particular incidences within the human domain.

In both humanities-oriented cases, information is considered basically as a human construction. It is the stance of so-called 'soft' science.

The most concrete classification might be along certain clusters of common perspectives.

A first cluster of information concepts/theories might be those that look upon information as a given. Sometimes this is called 'potential' information or 'structural' information. Structural sciences deal with this topic. According to them, matter is always in a certain shape, *gestalt*, form, and this form is information. Bernd-Olaf Küppers is a prominent advocate of this position which is espoused within the notion of *Strukturwissenschaften* (structural sciences), which was introduced in the 1970s by Carl Friedrich von Weizsäcker (Küppers, 2000).

A second cluster focuses on the transmission aspect. Seen from this angle, information does not lie in the structure but is transmitted from a sender to a receiver via a channel that is disturbed by noise. That is the classical view inaugurated by Shannon and Weaver which is considered the mother of all communication models (Shannon, 1948). What is said here to flow, to float, is sometimes called 'free' information.

A third and final cluster is that of the view of the receiver. Information is finally not that which is transmitted but that which is processed by the receiver. It is the receiver who, by processes of decoding, is considered to attach meaning to the message and to thereby produce 'actual' information. This is the leitmotif of all developments in communication studies, in particular, cultural studies, that try to complement, or depart from, the channel model.

So the range of information theories or concepts (and related phenomena) that, from a UTI point of view are to be subjected to an attempt of unification, is, according to the above classifications, as wide as that.

Q5. HOW CAN UNIFICATION BE ACHIEVED?

The review of the classifications of information concepts/theories so far seems to support the assumption that a multitude of approaches are diverse and irreconcilable and do not offer the possibility of consolidation. But on closer scrutiny, no matter where you start from—either from philosophy, two cultures, or the disciplinary point of departure—you will end up with one and the same scheme. From philosophy to scientific disciplines, the categorization of the existing information concepts/theories seems like a concretization and specification of the rather abstract and unifying classification in that the rather down-to-earth classes are embedded in the rather lofty classes. The clusters are embedded in the scientific cultures and the scientific cultures are embedded in philosophy. At each level, not between the levels, there is some discrepancy that forms an obstacle to unification.

According to the philosophical classification, information concepts are stuck between materialism and idealism, that is, they are stuck between the 'hard' and 'soft' side. But it does not come as a surprise that the 'hard' side is materialistic (like the philosophical inclination) and the 'soft' side idealistic. As for the clusters, 'information' seems to be exclusively 'potential' or exclusively 'free' or exclusively 'actual'. But the first and the second notion belong to the science and technology ('hard') side of the scientific divide, while the third notion has an affinity with the humanities ('soft') side.

How can this basic divide be bridged successfully?

How can matter, on the one hand, and idea, mind or information, on the other, be grasped as complements as well as information dealt with as a thing (a structure, a flow) or as a human construction (a processing activity)?

Taking into account that philosophy is not only about the essence or the nature or the substance of reality (ontology), but also about praxis (praxiology), we can ask whether or not the perspective of praxis provides us with a still more abstract view of information than the materialism-idealism divide already does, and we can ask to what extent this view can help us with unification through reworking and reinterpreting the classifications. If we assume that praxiology, ontology and epistemology form a kind of hierarchy (Hofkirchner *et al.*, 2005) with the praxiological point of view prior to the ontological point of view prior to the epistemological one, then we can ask the above questions.

Now, in praxiology, the point is to look upon everything in terms of objects and subjects and the relationships between them. Objects and subjects are defined by mutual exclusion. Objects are subject to subjects, subjects *subject* objects. Humans are subjects. Through interference with their human and non-human surroundings they produce objects. These objects tend to object to becoming subject to humans as there is inertia with them. Praxis is the ongoing process of subjecting objects to humans while factoring in inertia. Objects do not exist, unless subjects exist, and vice versa, and they are bound together by the process and relationship of praxis. This relationship is known as a dialectical one; a dialectical relationship is said to exist if the following criteria come true: firstly, both sides of the relationship are opposed to each other; secondly, they depend on each other; thirdly, they are asymmetrical in that neither side can be replaced by the other without replacing the mode of relationship simultaneously. Master-and-slave or mother-and-daughter are examples of dialectical relationships.

Now we recognize that the information concept/theory classifications presented above depend on how they view the object-subject-relationship.

According to the materialistic (as regards philosophy), 'hard' science (as regards the two cultures), and the structuralist and communicative stance (as regards the disciplines), we find that information is something objective. It seems not to belong to a subject and can be measured independently. According to the idealistic, 'soft' science and recipient's view, information is considered to be subjective, that is, inextricably linked to a subject that is human.

A UTI cannot be satisfied by such one-sided views. An integrative information science has to consider both the objective and subjective aspects of information and overcome objectivism and subjectivism as well.

The objectivist outlook is right in stating that information is a phenomenon that exists and is not merely human imagination. The subjectivist outlook is right insofar as it states that information occurs only if there is freedom of choice, to which the generation and disposal of information is attributed. However, regarding the objectivist outlook, we have to limit the scope of objects with which information is said to be found to those objects exclusively that take the role of subjects, and regarding the subjectivist outlook, we have to enlarge the sphere of subjects from that of humans exclusively and include non-human ones, too.

Since the materialism-idealism divide can be derived from the object-subject divide, in that matter is objective and ideas are subjective, it might become clear that matter and ideas belong together in the way that objects and subjects do.

An answer that goes beyond (materialistic and idealistic) monism and (if you like, interactive) dualism is dialectics. Dialectics recognize identity and difference of matter and information at the same time. They recognize identity, given the difference, for this identity makes it possible that these different sides interact. And they recognize the difference, given identity, for this makes it possible to differentiate matter and information as different specifications of an identical, common, genus. So in Emergentist Materialism, which is an example of this answer, matter is the common substance, but leaves room for emergent properties and events like the mind (information), which is of a different materiality compared with the simple, pure, materiality that occurs in the non-emergent state of matter (Bunge, 1980).

An answer that goes beyond the divide of the two cultures is a 'third' culture. Snow envisioned this third culture with the words:

> *With good fortune, however, we can educate a large proportion of our better minds so that they are not*

ignorant of imaginative experience, both in the arts and in
science, nor ignorant either of the endowments of applied
science, of the remediable suffering of most of their fellow
humans, and of the responsibilities which, once they are
seen, cannot be denied (Snow, 1998: 100).

According to John Brockman, the third culture is 'founded
on the realization of the import of complexity, of
evolution. Very complex systems—whether organisms,
brains, the biosphere, or the universe itself—were not
constructed by design; all have evolved' (Brockman, 1995:
20f). So information processes originated from evolution
and underwent evolution from early, rudimentary forms
to the advanced forms we face today. Social science
is the discontinuous continuation of natural science
inasmuch as the social forms of information processes
are the discontinuous continuation of natural forms of
information processes.

An answer that goes beyond the particularization of the
disciplinary clusters is that the third kind of categorization
turns out to run alongside the information processes
(processing). Altogether, the three clustered perspectives
seem to give a picture of a series of steps of information
processes. The first step, information frozen to a structure,
seems to represent something that might enter the
information process. The second step is then the leaking of
melted and liquefied information, the reaching out of the
'potential' information just by virtue of its showing up to
whatever is out there. And the third step, the 'actualization'
of the 'potential' information by an agency, could be seen
as a step in which the process is frozen again, but finds
itself in another structure, in a new structure of this very
agency (which, in turn, as new 'potential' information

might become a new starting point). Separately, however, these aspects can only account for a fragmented picture.

So the concept of information in a UTI is a concept that leaves the subject/object divide behind. It is a concept that is objective and subjective at the same time.

Q6. WHAT IS THE MEANING OF CAPURRO'S TRILEMMA WITH REGARD TO THE ATTEMPTS OF UNIFICATION?

Capurro's Trilemma runs like this (Capurro *et al.,* 1997): in attempting to define and determine what 'information' means throughout the disciplines (as well as in everyday thinking), and what it should or could mean, you face a logical situation that offers three options, none of which, however, is satisfactory (see Table 1).

information concepts	relationship between intension (meaning) and extension (fields)
synonymity	there is one singular meaning that applies to every field
analogy	there are several meanings similar to one particular meaning that serves as *primum analogatum*
equivocity	there are different meanings each of which applies to one singular field only

Table 1 *Capurro's Trilemma*

The first option is that there is only one meaning of the term 'information'; it means the same regardless of the field of application. This option is called synonymity, because the terms are synonyms.

The second option is that there are several meanings of the term 'information'; they are similar to a particular meaning, which serves as a standard of comparison. This option is called analogy, analogical reasoning, because the terms are analogies.

The third option is that there are several meanings of the term 'information', all of which are different from each other. This option is called equivocity, because the terms are equivocations.

No option actually, meets the demands of scientificity. Synonymity does not meet them, because information in one domain would not differ from information in a different domain; a premise which has long been contested. Analogical reasoning does not meet them either, because there is no agreement on the *primum analogatum*, the standard of comparison. Nor does equivocity meet them, because the Babel of languages which are not communicable would mean the end of all scientific enterprise .

Does this mean that we are stuck and that there is no solution to the trilemma?

No. The three options Capurro's Trilemma offers are tantamount to three well-defined ways of thinking: the black, the white and the black-and-white way of thinking; that is, the reductive, the projective and the disjunctive way. But there is a fourth way of thinking; the integrative one (see Table 2).

What is a way of thinking? A way of thinking is the way how identity and difference are thought to relate to each other. Relating identity and difference may be presumed to be the most basic function of thinking. That is, practical problems that come to thought, entities that are investigated, phenomena that have to be recognized, may be identical in certain respects but may differ from each other in other respects.

ways of thinking	relationship between lower and higher complexity
reductionism	reduces higher complexity to lower complexity
projectivism	projects higher complexity onto lower complexity
disjunctivism	disjoins higher complexity from lower complexity
integrativism	integrates lower complexity into higher complexity which it differentiates from the former

Table 2 *Ways of Thinking*

With regard to identity and difference, given complexity, that is, provided that what is more complex is more differentiated but simultaneously more integrated, the question arises as to how the simple relates to the complex; that is, how less complex problems or objects or phenomena relate to more complex ones.

The first way of thinking, in terms of ideal types, establishes identity by eliminating the difference for the benefit of the less complex side of the difference and at the cost of the more complex side; it reduces 'higher complexity' to 'lower complexity'. This is known as reductionism. Reductionism is still the main stream of natural science.

The counterpart of the reductive way of thinking is what might be called projective. Projective thinking also establishes identity by eliminating the difference, albeit for the benefit of the more complex side of the difference and at the cost of the less complex side. It takes the 'higher' level of complexity as its point of departure and extrapolates or projects from there to the 'lower' level of complexity. It overestimates the role of the whole and belittles the role of the parts. This is one trait of the humanities.

Both the reductive and the projective ways of thinking yield unity without diversity.

There is a third way, opposed to both of the others, which eliminates identity by establishing the difference for the sake of each manifestation of complexity in its own right. It abandons all relationships between all of them by treating them as disjunctive; it dissociates one from the other; it dichotomizes and yields dualism (or pluralism) in the sense of diversity without unity. Let's call it 'disjunctivism'. The often bemoaned gap between the so-called two cultures of hard science and soft science (humanities) is the most striking example of this way of thinking. In fact, this is a description of the state of the scientific adventure as a multiplicity of mono-disciplinary approaches that are alien and deaf to each other.

You can see easily that the options of synonymity, analogy and equivocity are reductive, projective and disjunctive respectively.

Either you have unity without diversity (in the first and second case) or you have diversity without unity (in the third case). What is needed, however, is *unitas multiplex* as French philosopher and sociologist Edgar Morin calls it (1999: 25); understanding unity-in-diversity and diversity-in-unity; unity-through-diversity.

> *It means understanding disjunctive, reductive thought by exercising thought that distinguishes and connects. It does*

not mean giving up knowledge of the parts for knowledge of the whole, or giving up analysis for synthesis, it means conjugating them. This is the challenge of complexity which ineluctably confronts us as our planetary era advances and evolves (Morin, 1999: 19).

This is a way of thinking that establishes identity as well as difference, favouring neither of the manifestations of complexity. It establishes identity in line with the difference, integrates both sides of the difference (yielding unity), and differentiates identity (yielding diversity). It is a way of thinking based upon integration and differentiation and is opposed to both dissociation and unification and yields unity and diversity in one. It integrates 'lower' and 'higher complexity' by establishing a dialectical relationship between them.

This integrativism opposes reductionism and projectivism, as well as disjunctivism.

The unity-through-diversity principle is itself a kind of dialectical sublation of unification and dissociation, of reductionism and projectivism and disjunctivism. A dialectical sublation eliminates the dominant role of the preceding quality rather than the quality itself. This quality is kept, that is, continued, but is continued under the dominance of a new quality and is therefore, as Hegel put it, lifted onto the next level. All of that holds for the unity-through-diversity thinking with regard to the fallacious ways of thinking. Reductionism, projectivism, as well as disjunctivism, are not totally negated but taken *cum grano salis*. Each of them has an aspect of overexaggeration that has to be abolished but, by the same token, they have an aspect that is right once the one-sidedness is removed.

Doing justice to these aspects is carried out through the novel integrative view, in such a way that unity is established among the diverse confligating views.

To sum up, reduction, projection or duality are justified within certain boundaries, when taking into account the legitimate claims of each other. This is the integrative way of thinking that a UTI has to carry out.

Q7. IS A UTI SIMILAR TO A GRAND UNIFIED THEORY (GUT) OR A THEORY OF EVERYTHING (TOE)?

Yes and no.

Yes, insofar as both the UTI and the GUT/TOE aim to provide a bigger picture. The UTI seeks for understanding different manifestations of information processes in the universe, just as the GUT/TOE tries to find a common denominator for the four fundamental interactions/forces gravitation, electromagnetism, the weak and the strong (quantum chromodynamics) interaction/force.

But if the GUT/TOE is meant only as a pure physical theory for the explanation of physical phenomena or as a physical theory which gives final explanations of phenomena other than physical in the universe, then the answer is 'no'. A UTI is not a pure physical theory and information is not a pure physical phenomenon (like interaction/force), which Carles Seife (2007) insinuates, and the properties of information that go beyond physicality in that they extend to living beings and to social human life are not expected to be explained in terms of mere physics.

A UTI is not a physicalistic and hence reductionistic theory which yields a world formula, that allows for explanations and predictions by subsumption under a general and hence abstract construct.

A world formula does not prove feasible, and a unified concept of information is not a world formula.

What a UTI searches for is a concept as abstract as necessary but as concrete as possible at the same time.

On the one hand, the concept will theorize what all information processes have in common, but it will not be reduced to an abstract formalism that can subsume every case under a meaningless meaning.

On the other hand, it will cover each individual information process that may empirically be found but not hypostatize its unique particularities into a concretistic notion.

This is the real challenge. We need a concept that is flexible enough to balance the universal and the particular, to do justice to both of them, to relate them so as to render the universal in need, as well as capable of being completed by the particular and, in turn, embed the particular in the universal (Hofkirchner, 2004).

Reductionistic unification would reduce the particular to the universal by stating, 'The Particular is (nothing but) Universal' and assuming that the universal is the necessary, as well as sufficient, condition for the particular. This is true of all kinds of subsumption, which overlook what goes beyond that which subsumes. Unification by projection would project the particular onto the universal and postulate 'The Universal is (nothing but) Particular', thereby meaning that the particular is not only necessary but also sufficient to yield the universal. This holds for those illusions that extend what is in common to a realm where it is not. The disjunctive way of thinking would dissociate the particular from the universal by presuming 'The Particular and the Universal are Disjoint', and would, therefore, insinuate that both notions contradict each other. This leads to letting the particular fall apart, since there is no unifying bond. Either one of these three ways of thinking is one-sided because, by relying on the formal-logical figure of necessary and sufficient conditions or of contradiction, they focus on the mutual dependence of the sides or on being opposites, and do not comprise the full range of what is characteristic of any dialectical relation.

It is only the fourth way of thinking that integrates, as well as differentiates, the particular and universal. This point of view may be formulated as 'The Particular Sublates the Universal'; 'sublation' in the threefold Hegelian sense, denoting suspending, saving and elevating:

- The particular suspends the universal. As the opposite of the universal, the particular contradicts the universal and transcends it;

- The particular saves the universal. The particular depends on the universal, the latter being the necessary, but not sufficient condition for the particular. The particular is based upon the universal, and;

- The particular elevates the universal to another level. In an asymmetrical effort, the particular turns the universal, as a consequence, from an abstract universal into a concrete-universal.

The concrete-universal is the unity that overarches the diversity of the particular. Aristotle paved the way for the dialectics of the universal and the particular by establishing specification hierarchies via *genus proximum* and *differentia specifica*. The whole tree can be considered to represent the concrete-universal, and each ramification to specify one particular instantiation of the universal by making the abstract concrete.

Specification hierarchies of being are the logical way of grasping the history and genesis of becoming (unity of being and becoming).

In this way, a UTI seeks a concrete-universal concept of information rather than an abstract one.

Q8. IS INFORMATION POSSIBLE IN A MECHANISTIC UNIVERSE?

Newton's mechanical perception of the world was based on three principles (Gerthsen *et al.*, 1995: 13; Fleissner *et al.*, 1997):

- The principle of inertia: a body on which no forces are exerted moves constantly in a straight line.

- The principle of action: If a force *F* is exerted on a body of mass *m* and velocity *v*, the impulse of the body, *mv*, is changed, such that d/dt (*mv*) = *F*. From *F* = 0 follows the above principle of inertia.

- The principle of reaction: If the force *F* which is acting on a body has its origin in another body, exactly the opposite force *-F* is acting on the latter.

Newton's classical mechanics used the concept of causality in an elementary way. If a force is acting on a body, by the principle of action the velocity of the body is changed in a unique way. The body is accelerated proportionately to the force exerted.

These principles imply the unique determination of the effect on the basis of a known cause. Newton's writings became *the* prototype for scientific reasoning, establishing determinism by eradicating other types of cause than efficient cause.

This mechanistic worldview was made explicit by the well-known idea of Laplace, that a demon who knew the world formula, plus all data describing a certain state of the universe, would be capable of predicting and retro-dicting any state of the universe, which in Popper's terms may be called the clockwork view of the universe (Popper, 1966).

The thesis of strict determinism, in terms of systems, can be characterized as follows (Heylighen, 1990; Weingartner, 1996: 187–89):

- Given a system, inputs and outputs are related in such a way that each input is related to one, and only one, output. The system transforms the input into the output by way of a mechanism which can be conceived of as a bijection. If you call the input 'cause' and the output 'effect', you may state that equal causes have equal effects and distinct causes have distinct effects.
- Small changes in the causes lead to small changes in the effects.
- There are only repetitions. Each state of a system will return in the future.

This assumption is visualized in Figure 2 where the set of causes is mapped to the set of effects in a bijective way.

In this sense *causa aequat effectum* or, as Newton's dictum was interpreted elsewhere, *actio est reactio* (Fleissner *et al.*, 1997). Owing to the mathematical function, a tool is provided by which calculable results seem to be guaranteed.

Therefore, a clockwork universe offers no room for information. If we presume that information has something to do with novelty, information is not possible

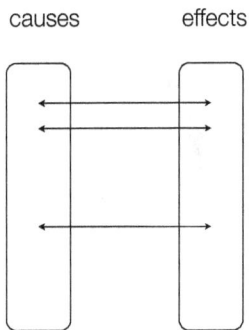

causes   effects

Figure 2 *Strict Determinism*

in a mechanistic universe because there is nothing new to this universe. There is also no need for a concept of information. Everything can be explained in terms of matter. Specific conditions of matter instantiate universal laws of matter. The only place where information could enter the stage is the case of human knowledge about these laws. Science would then be the historical process by which absolute truth is revealed; an idea that is definitely out-of-date.

Q9. WHAT CAN WE LEARN FROM THE NEW PARADIGM OF COMPLEXITY?

Today, there is a paradigm shift from classical physics towards self-organization theories, and from the mechanistic worldview which originally laid the foundations for classical physics, towards a view which allows for processes that produce emergent properties, relations and entities (Kanitscheider, 1993; Coveney *et al.*, 1990; Goerner, 1994). It is worth mentioning the remarkable words of Sir James Lighthill (1986), who regretted that so many scientists had, for so many centuries trailed what, in the 1960s, was proven definitely false. He felt obliged to apologize publicly for this.

Heinz von Foerster is known as the first who, at the end of the 1950s, introduced the notion of self-organizing systems to the scientific community (though this notion then had a somewhat different and restricted meaning). In 1960, von Foerster published the article 'On Self-Organizing Systems and its Environment', one of the first and most important works on this topic (von Foerster, 1995). In 1961, he organized a conference on self-organizing systems in Chicago and, together with George Zopf, he edited the proceedings in 1962 (von Foerster *et al.*, 1962).

With the transition from System Theory I to System Theory II, as with the change from Cybernetics I to Cybernetics II and the increased slope of the Theory of Evolution which overcomes the restrictions of the Darwinian model, we can see a theory of open, non-linear, complex, dynamic, self-

organizing (in short: evolutionary) systems approaching.
This theory no longer deals merely with mechanisms,
strategies and controls for achieving/maintaining
homeostasis and the development of species. It concerns
the rise and fall of real-world systems. The concepts
of dissipative structures, synergetics, hyper-cycles,
autopoeisis and self-referentiality are the most prominent
predecessors of a theory of evolutionary systems.
These deal with manifold topics like the formation of
structures by means of coherent behavior of particles in
thermodynamics or laser-active materials, the formation
of spatial or temporal patterns in chemical reactions, the
origin and development of highly complex molecules
as prerequisites for the formation of biotic systems,
phylogenesis (in which the adaptation of systems to their
changing environments is seen as the achievement of the
systems themselves rather than the achievement of the
environment as implied by old evolutionary theories) and
ontogenesis, the relation of matter and mind and cultural
phenomena.

As science has unravelled the natural world, mechanical
relations and strict determinism which are prevalent in
the clockwork view of the universe hold for systems at, or
nearly at, thermodynamic/chemical equilibrium only. But
they do not hold for systems exposed to fields in which the
uneven distribution of energy density exceeds a critical
level. Such field potentials force energy to flow in non-
linear and interdependent ways. And here the systems
reveal self-organization; that is, the build-up of order out
of fluctuations via dissipation of entropy.

Self-organization may be looked upon as the way
evolutionary systems come into existence or change their

structure, state or behavior and the way they maintain themselves (their structure, state or behavior). In either case, it is a process in which a difference is produced or reproduced, in which a quality, which differs from the qualities that existed before a certain point of time, is made to appear or, from that point on, is sustained vis-à-vis and by virtue of the coexisting qualities from which it differs. So, in either case, emergence is the underlying process.

Thus a philosophy of emergence seems the proper background theory for evolutionary systems thinking. Emergentist philosophy, as developed, for instance, by Lewis Morgan and summed up by David Blitz (1992) in a book on Emergent Evolution, holds that effects which do not 'result' from causes—which are not 'resultant' but 'emergent'—cannot be 'reduced' to their causes. In this case, causation is only a necessary constraint, but not a sufficient one as it is in mechanistic causation.

By that, self-organization inheres a touch of spontaneity, a touch of indeterminacy, since the order that is built up is not determined fully. Bifurcations mark possibilities for the system to go one way or another in building up its order. But there is no condition outside the system that compels the system to go this way or that. It is up to the system itself. It is determined that the system has to go one way or another, but it is not determined in which way the system has to go.

In case of less-than-strict determinism and emergentism causality, in terms of system-theoretical considerations, in contradistinction to the description of a mechanical universe, must be described as follows (Hofkirchner, 1998):

- Inputs and outputs are not related in a way which can be plotted as bijective mapping. There are no transformation mechanisms which unambiguously turn the causes into the effects; causes and effects are coupled in a way that allows different causes to have the same effect and the same cause to have different effects;

- Small changes in the causes may lead to big changes in the effects, and;

- The more complex a system, the less probable the return of a certain state in the future.

This is what ensues ontologically from findings in self-organization research, and is presented in Figure 3.

Thus *causa non aequat effectum, actio non est reactio*. Owing to mathematical shortcuts not being applicable, emergent phenomena cannot be predicted in detail. There is no mechanistic transformation which turns the cause into the effect. There is an activity of the system itself which selects one of the several possible ways of reacting. There remains a gap in quality between cause and effect which cannot be bridged in a mechanical way.

Hence, standing on the base of the concept of emergence, we have, on the one hand, the opportunity to stick to the principle of causality, which means that there is nothing which was created out of nothing (let's leave the question of the coming into being of the universe out) and, on the other hand, there remains enough openness to let novelties arise which did not exist before.

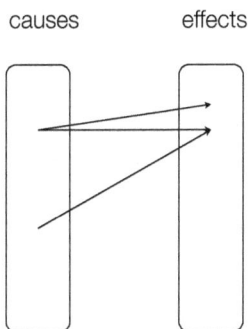

Figure 3 *Less-Than-Strict Determinism*

Less-than-strict determinism is not to say that there is no determinism at all, or that the clockwork view has to be replaced with a cloud's view. It does not mean that anything goes. It only admits that nature itself is capable of producing events spontaneously which are not describable in a mechanistic way and that, besides and beyond clear-cut one-to-one cause-effect-relations, there are more flexible causal connections in the real world, too, which seem to be more important and greater in number. These connections are due to the fact that self-organizing systems have the freedom to choose between several alternatives (see Figure 4), compared with mechanical systems where there is only one possibility (see Figure 5). Seen in this way, strict determinacy is but a special case of causality. It applies if, and only if, the system is deprived of the freedom to choose between several alternatives.

In this way, the thesis of less-than-strict determinism not only opposes the thesis of strict determinism but also leads to a new understanding of determinism, which includes strictness as correct only under certain conditions.

The common feature of all non-mechanical causation is that the cause is an event which plays the role of a mere trigger of processes, which themselves depend on the nature of the system (at least as much as they are dependent on the influence from the system's environment), and that the effect is an event in which this very self-organization process finally ends up.

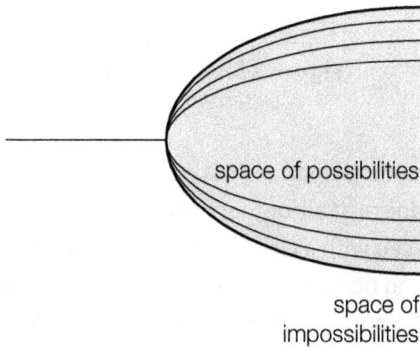

Figure 4 *Trajectories in Self-Organizing Systems*

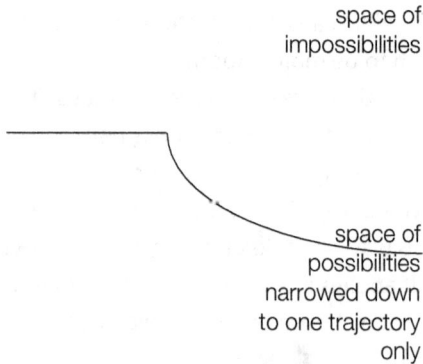

Figure 5 *Trajectories in Mechanical Systems*

Q10. HOW IS INFORMATION RELATED TO SELF-ORGANIZATION?

Actually, with the paradigm shift from the mechanistic worldview, that knows only objects towards a more inclusive view of a less-than-strict, emergent, and even creative universe inhabited by subjects too, we have got everything required to connect the notion of information to the idea of self-organization. It is the very idea of systems intervening between input/cause and output/effect and thus breaking up the direct cause-effect-relationships of the mechanistic worldview that facilitates, if not demands, the notion of information, for information is bound to the precondition of subjects and their subjective agency. Self-organizing systems that transform the input into an output in a non-mechanical way, in the context of an amount of degrees of freedom undeniably greater than that of a one-option only, are subjects. And each activity in such a context, each acting vis-à-vis undeniable degrees of freedom, is nothing less than the generation of information because the act to discriminate, distinguish, differentiate, is information.

Self-organization stands, therefore, at the beginning of all information, insofar:

- As the system selects one of a number of possible responses to a causal event in its environment;

- As it shows preference for the particular option it chooses to realize over a number of other options, and;

- As it decides to discriminate.

So we can say that information is involved in self-organization. Every system acts and reacts in a network of systems, elements and networks, and is exposed to influences mediated by matter and/or energy relations. If the effects on the system are fully derivable from, and fully reducible to, the causes outside the system, no informational aspects can be separated from matter/energy cause-effect relations. However the system produces information, as soon as the effects become dependent on the system as well (because the system itself contributes to them); as soon as the influences play the role of mere triggers for effects being self-organized by the system; as soon as degrees of freedom intervene and the reaction of the system is unequal to the action it undergoes (Haken, 1988). Information is created if there is a surplus of effects exceeding causes in a system. Information occurs during the process in which the system exhibits changes in its structure, its state or its behavior (Fenzl et al., 1996), that is, changes which are a result of the system. Information is created by a system if it is organizing itself at any level. Information is that part of the process of self-organization that is responsible for generating new features in the system's structure, state or behavior. In a figurative sense, information can be looked upon as the result of this process, as what is new in the structure, state or behavior. And insofar as this new feature in system A may serve to stimulate self-organizing (and therefore informational) processes to produce new features in system B, we can speak of information in a metaphoric sense, as if it were something to be sent from one system to another.

Summing up, we can speak of information in the following situations: where the deterministic connection between cause and effect is broken up; where a system's own activity comes into play, and the cause becomes the mere trigger of self-determined processes in the system, which finally lead to the effect; where the system makes a decision and a possibility is realized by an irreducible choice.

Since information generation is a process that allows novelty to emerge, it is worth noting that it is not a mechanical process that can be formalized, expressed by a mathematical function or carried out by a computer.

The concept of information thus stimulates the meaning it had before it was reduced to a term denoting simply a message, as the Greek *aggelia* did. Originally, *informatio* in Latin meant not just the result of an action or a process, but the action/process as well, namely *informare* (Capurro, 1978). *In-formare* meant 'to bring into form, give shape to', and the subject could be man, with man or nature as object, the subject could be nature with man or nature itself as object, and the subject could be God with man or nature as object (see Table 3). This notion sounds astonishingly modern if we see humans as part of nature and assume that God does not intervene in natural processes; an anticipation of the very concept of self-organization today. To the ancient thinkers the forms which gave shape to matter used to mark differences in quality, that is, in-forming meant a process, as a result of which something new appeared.

subject	object	activity
man	man	to educate
	nature	to design
nature	man	to imprint
	nature	to produce
god	man	to teach
	nature	to shape

Table 3 *The Ancient Concept of Informatio/Informare*

Q11. WHAT IS THE ROLE OF SIGN PROCESSES IN A UTI?

Information occurs when the system organizes itself in one way or another and, to use a semiotic term, 'interprets' the difference in its environment by virtue of its own activity. What does this mean? Is it justified to introduce a semiotic term (semiotics deals with semiosis which means sign processes)?

The essential point to grasp here is that a difference in the environment does make a difference to the system, as Gregory Bateson (1972) defined information. A difference in the environment makes a difference to the system, if it triggers a self-organization process in which the system builds up some new order. The system does this in relation to the trigger, it relates this order to the trigger, it 'interprets' the order as the trigger. Information generation is that activity of the system that builds up order by which the system 'interprets' that which triggered the activity.

So we have a tripartite relation. Information is:

- Something (the self-organized ordering);
- About another thing (the trigger), and;
- To a third thing (the system itself).

And this is exactly what, in semiotics, is understood by a sign.

What is a sign? In everyday life the following definition seems widely used; a sign is something that stands for something else. It can be argued that this common-sense definition is appropriate and capable of development in scientific respect, too. Traditionally, in science, a sign is defined, on the one hand, by dyadic semiotic schools, either as a unity of carrier and meaning, or as a unity of carrier and object and, on the other hand, by triadic schools as a unity of carrier, meaning and object together, whatever the terms for the correlatives may be (Nöth, 2000: 136-41).

Since we have a tripartite relation, triadic semiotics rather than dyadic semiotics seem to qualify for contributing to a UTI.

In both cases, however, the notion of sign is linked implicitly to the notion of subject. For speaking of a carrier that conveys meaning or refers to an object requires speaking of a subject, too. Only if a subject is assumed, does it makes sense to assume something as a carrier of meaning, because that something is not a carrier unless it serves a subject. Moreover, only if a subject is assumed, does it make sense to assume something like meaning, because meaning is always meaning to some subject. Last but not least, only if a subject is assumed, does it make sense to assume an object, because things are not objects until they are subject to a subject.

Therefore, it makes sense to revisit the traditional semiotic triangle from the viewpoint of a subject-object dialectics.

The subject-object dialectics can be visualized by a cycle by which the subject couples up to the object (see Figure 6).

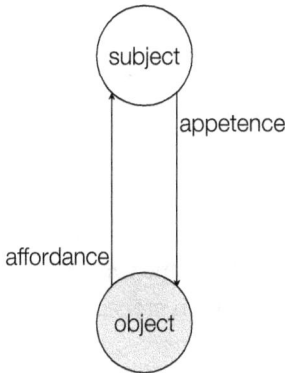

Figure 6 *Subject-Object Dialectic*

On the one hand, the object bears significance to the subject insofar as its objective properties are able to suit subjective functions—this is called 'affordance' elsewhere (Gibson, 1979)—and, on the other, the subject designates the object for serving it one way or another because it needs to reach out for that which it makes into an object and needs to approach the object in a subjective way. In a different context, this is called 'appetence'.

It is in this very relationship that we find the origins of information: because of subjective appetence relating to objective affordance we have subjective signification relating to objective significance. 'Signification' and 'significance' describe a field of latency for information to emerge. It is this relationship by which a subject relates itself to an object via its own activity from which information emerges.

Now we have to take into consideration that a subject never relates directly to an object. Its relation to the object is always mediated. It construes the means of mediation.

In the course of the subject's acting upon the object the subject gives rise to something new by which it mediates itself with the object; the sign (see Figure 7). The sign is a means for the subject to bring together its appetence for the object, that is, the signification it attributes to the object, with the affordance of the object, that is, the significance the object has for the subject. The appearance of the sign *(signans)* turns the subject into a signmaker *(signator);* the signification process *(significatio)* into a designation process *(designatio),* which means that the signification process is sign-mediated; and the object into something (to be) signified *(signandum/signatum)* that bears a significance for the subject *(significantia).*

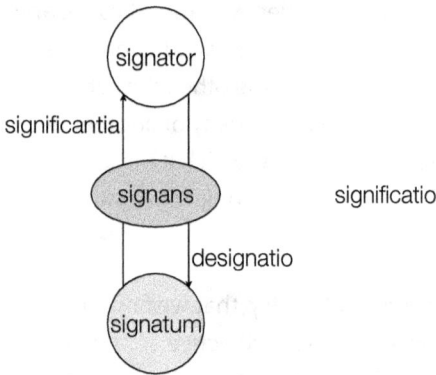

Figure 7 *Designation as Sign-Mediated Subject-Object Dialectic*

If we want to sketch this relationship in the traditional form of a semiotic triangle, we arrive at the following picture (Figure 8): the subject *(signator)* generates and utilizes the sign. The object is that part of the relationship for which a sign is (to be) produced *(signandum/signatum).* And the sign is a product of the subject's own activity that stands for the object *(signans).* The interference of the sign makes the process, in which a signification is attributed to the object *(significatio)*, a process of assigning a sign to the object that conveys the signification *(designatio)*.

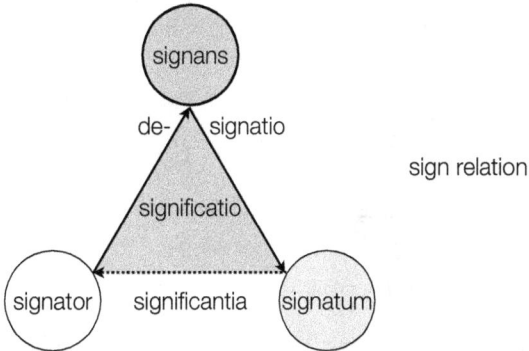

Figure 8 *A Semiotic Triangle Compatible with Subject-Object Dialectic*

The triangle is made up of the three correlatives signmaker *(signator)*, (to be) signified *(signandum/signatum)* and sign *(signans)*. However, it has to be stressed that there is no relation between *signandum/signatum* and *signans*, unless there is a *signator* that establishes the relation. It is even more important to point out that after the sign relation has been established, the *signator's* interchange with the *signatum* is *signans*-mediated and henceforth channelled by the *signans*. The *signans*, once emerged, is the new quality that exerts dominance over the *signator's* relation to the *signatum*.

It is worth noting that the triangle sketched here is different from the traditional semiotic triangle. Triadic semiotics in the tradition of Charles Sanders Peirce (1983, 2000) know the 'object', the *'representamen'* (the sign in a narrow sense) and the 'interpretant', which is different from the interpreter and means the 'meaning' of the *representamen*. There are some current attempts at integrating the semiotics of Peirce into modern evolutionary thought and modern systems thinking (e.g., Taborsky, 2001; the Danish school of Biosemiotics with Hoffmeyer, 1996; Emmeche, 1998; Brier, 1999 & 2008). This does not come as a surprise, as Peirce himself was an evolutionary thinker (Hausman, 1993).

In order, however, to be able to merge evolutionary systems thinking with semiotics we have to make use of the revised triangle. According to this, a sign is:

- Something;
- That stands for another thing, and;
- It does so to a third thing.

This is analogous to the tripartite definition of information.

Then we can proceed in saying that the something is the self-organized order of the system, the other thing is an event or a condition in the umwelt of the system, and the third thing is the respective evolving system.

And we can conclude that it seems sensible to use the terms 'information' and 'sign', as well as 'information process' and 'semiosis' interchangeably.

According to this unifying perspective, information is the relation of self-organizing systems to their environment. In terms of evolutionary systems theory, information is generated if self-organizing systems relate some external 'perturbation' (that is how Maturana and Varela in their theory of autopoeisis are inclined to term the input from the outside) to the spontaneous build-up of order they execute when exposed to this perturbation. To translate into terms of triadic semiotics, by doing so, the self-organizing systems assign a signification to the order and make it a sign which stands for the thus signified perturbation.

Q12. HOW CAN WE DIFFERENTIATE SELF-ORGANIZATION?

From the viewpoint of the new paradigm in science, the historical development of the physical, as well as the philosophical concept of causality, may be looked upon as step-by-step efforts to overcome the limits of mechani(ci)sm (Mainzer, 1994). Leibniz was among the first, but not the last to oppose the philosophical mechanistic principle (for an in-depth examination of Leibniz, see Holz, 1983), which was then propagated in the aftermath of Descartes. Kant and Schelling are often mentioned in this context (for Schelling as a precursor of self-organization theoreticians, see Heuser-Kessler, 1992). Political, economic, social and ideological circumstances in the dawning age of industrialism impeded those efforts which focused on integration, unification and synthesis (rather than differentiation, particularization and analysis). Only today, in the face of global challenges to the survival of humanity, does the fragmented way of thinking seem to become obsolete.

Speaking of subjectiveness means returning to the terms 'subject' and 'object'. According to the praxio-onto-epistemological point of view, the difference between subject and object may be seen in the way that a subject is capable of determining itself while an object is not. An object is something that is determined by something that is not itself. Being a subject supersedes being merely an object. While an object has no possibility of acting in ways different from merely reacting to external determinants, a subject is capable of responding on its own, unequivocal way; that is, it can make use of degrees of freedom, of freedom of choice, of choice between options all of which it disposes of and thus makes the internal determine. It may object to external determinants in a subjective way that objects are not capable of.

So, if an object is something that is subject to mere determination by something else, and if a subject is something that objects to mere determination by something else, then information-generating, self-organizing systems display a certain subjectiveness, for the generation of information is tantamount with drawing a self-made distinction by the irreproducible, irreversible, irreducible, unpredictable build-up of order during the process of self-organization.

The minimal unit of subjectiveness is something that is provided with a minimal quantum of degrees of freedom to act. This something is the most rudimentary and primitive subject. It is already a somebody, albeit not a human one, and also not a living one.

It is not only less-than-strict determinism that is necessary to allow for subjectiveness. It is also more than effect-entailing causes that are characteristic of subjects of all kinds.

Aristotle knew four types of causes: the effective *(causa efficiens),* the final *(causa finalis),* the material *(causa materialis)* and the formal *(causa formalis).* In a strive for scientificity that avoided resorting to the supernatural, post-medieval science abandoned the last three. However, in the perspective of evolution and systems it is worth reconsidering all four types of causes, without need to resort to the supernatural. We can sort them into two pairs of opposites and arrange them on two continuum scales that stand orthogonally to each other (see Figure 9). One axis shows the dynamic dimension of systemic evolution and goes from driveness to end-directedness. Another shows the hierarchic dimension of evolutionary systems and goes from materiality to formative power (Brunner *et al.*, 2003). We can arrange the effective and final cause on the first axis, and the material and formal cause on the second one in the following way: effective cause enters the picture from the left and final cause as opposed to effective cause is directed to the left, which means that the more we move to the right on the x-axis, the less important is effective cause and the more important is final cause. Material cause enters the picture from the bottom and formal cause, as opposed to material cause, is directed to the bottom which means that the more we move to the top on the y-axis, the less important is material cause and the more important is formal cause.

Effective cause connotes a driving force in the process while final cause connotes pulling rather than pushing. But final cause enters the picture from the left too and

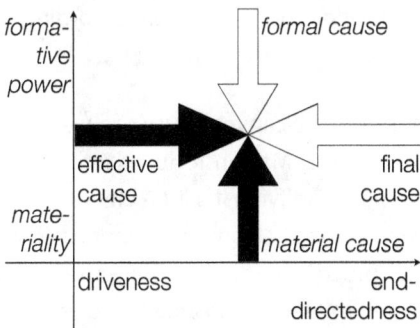

Figure 9 *Aristotle's Four Causes Revisited*

not from the right. Finality does mean influence 'from the future' as little as effectivity means exerting pressure 'from the past'. Each process paves the way for the future by its own history. It brings into existence a certain range of possibilities and a complementary range of impossibilities. Those possibilities do exist in the present and one of them will be selected and realized and then open up another range of possibilities. Compared to the range of impossibilities, the process converges to one end after the other, through a series of concatenated ranges of possibilities.

And material cause connotes the substantial base in the structure while formal cause connotes the shaping of it. Formal cause enters the picture from the bottom too though its direction is top-down. It does not fall from heaven. Formality means influence 'by mind' as little as materiality means exerting pressure 'by matter'. Each structure bears the stamp of how its constituents are composed. The constituents produce what they constitute by producing constraints as well as enablers, which represent the form.

Having made these assumptions, we are able to identify subjects of all kinds and locate them according to the axes (see Figure 10).

As to the first axis, we can make use of a well-known distinction that Ernst Mayr introduced into the theory of biology while modifying it a little bit (1974). He distinguished among 'teleomatic', 'teleonomic' and 'teleological' processes. The first evoke an analogy to automatic, and the second an analogy to economic processes. According to Mayr, teleomatic processes end up

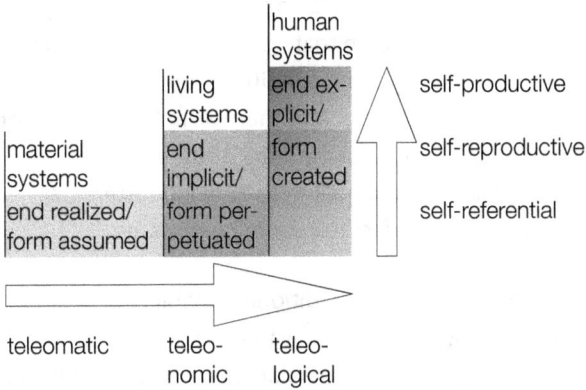

Figure 10 *Typology of Self-Organizing Systems According to the Rise of Subjectiveness*

as a consequence of physical laws like in gravity, entropy, decay, reaction gradients. Processes are teleonomic owing to an in-built programme which directs them towards an end as in homeostasis, ontogeny, biotic reproduction. Teleological processes can be found with the intervention of cognitive mechanisms, mostly human.

In Mayr, teleomatic processes are strictly mechanical, that is, they can be described and explained in terms of strict determinism. But with the new paradigm it became apparent that there are more interesting systems than pure mechanical systems and these are self-organizing systems. With them there is an end to which these systems tend; it is implicit and internal, but its conditions for satisfaction depend almost wholly on external conditions. We propose reserving the category of teleomatic only for processes in these primitive, physical and chemical, self-organizing systems (with Bénard convection cells or Belousov-Zhabotinsky reaction waves as the most prominent examples, see e.g. Bishop, 2008).

Let's go one step further. Teleonomic systems go beyond mere teleomatic ones in that, to a certain degree, they can exert control over the conditions for meeting an end which itself is being built into them or, at least, given from the outside to them (Coulter *et al.,* 1982: 43). Since survival is an end that is being built-in to all living systems, all living systems manifest teleonomic processes.

And another step is the additional capability of setting goals, of constructing ends by the systems in question. We propose to reserve this capability for human systems only and to use the term 'teleological' for them exclusively.

By that we have a clear-cut logical distinction between, firstly, systems and processes that result in an end when conditions are met, secondly, systems and processes that have an in-built end and can control the conditions to meet it, and, thirdly, systems and processes that construe a diversity of ends.

Let's look at the second axis. Here, we propose to introduce similar steps. There are systems and processes that manifest patterns. Pattern is form, that is, a superstructure that refers to a basis that refers to the superstructure, and so on. These are macro- and micro-levels that coexist and influence each other, which are more important than the influence from outside. The system is produced by its elements and the system constrains and enables its elements at the same time. As this works by dissipation of entropy, Ilya Prigogine (1980) called the emerging structures 'dissipative'. The fluid particle in the Bénard convection cell is prompted to contribute to the cell structure which emerges from the activities of all particles.

Then, there are systems and processes that are able to maintain the form they show, that is, to hold the form stable while matter is changing. This is the case with all living systems. Maturana and Varela (1980) called them 'autopoietic' in order to denote the fact that they are systems that produce themselves by constraining and enabling their elements to produce new elements that produce the systems.

Finally, there are systems and processes that change their form in a rather deliberative way, that is, they transcend and invent themselves. This is what Erich Jantsch (1987) was pointing at when he talked of 're-creative' systems at the human level. Think of different societal formations (e.g. capitalism, communism), of different party programmes transformed into Government plans for transforming society, of individual life-planning and different projects that individuals carry out by which they try to become what they want to be.

We propose to call them self-referential, self-reproductive (in the theoretical sense of producing the conditions required to maintain itself), and self-productive ('productivity' going beyond the Maturana-Varela 'poiesis') respectively.

It turns out that all self-organizing systems can be considered to be teleomatic as to the end-directedness and self-referential as to the formative power, that all biotic self-organizing systems are that subset of self-organizing systems that are, in addition, teleonomic regarding the end-directedness and self-reproductive regarding the formative power, and that all social systems are that subset of biotic self-organizing systems that are, in addition, teleological with regard to the end-directedness and self-productive with regard to the formative power.

Thus, we can discern degrees of subjectiveness. We can depict simple dissipative systems as proto-subjects, and simple autopoietic systems as quasi-subjects while reserving the property of being a subject in the full sense of the word for recreative systems only. But there is a continuum in the evolution of subjectiveness.

Q13. PATTERN FORMATION IN MATERIAL SYSTEMS— IS IT GENERATION OF INFORMATION?

Yes, it is. The most primitive sign manifestation is to be found with the most primitive kind of self-organization processes, that is, in processes by which systems (re)structure themselves and establish a feedback loop between their micro- and macro-levels. Systems that are capable of this kind of self-referentiality are so-called dissipative systems. Thermodynamically speaking, they dissipate the entropy that is the by-product of performing work when (re)structuring. In performing work they degrade energy and they succeed in getting rid of it which is necessary to qualify the building of the new structure as the generation of a higher order rather than a degeneration of the system. The process of (re) structuration ends up in a spatial and/or temporal pattern. The pattern is the distinction that is drawn by the system.

On this stage of physical- and chemical-systems evolution there is no differentiation among the three levels of system structure, system state and system behavior. That is to say, these systems only exhibit self-organization in a dissipative, thermodynamic way. There is only one transformation function, that is, one cycle of self-organization. The new structure is, thus, identical to the new state of the system and also to its new behavior (Atmanspacher *et al.*, 1990; Atmanspacher *et al.*, 1992; Haken, 1988). Therefore, there is no differentiation among the three semiosic aspects either. The syntactical, semantic and pragmatic aspects of information coincide. However, in the pattern *in nuce* all three semiosic relations can be found:

- The syntactical aspect comes to the fore because there is not an unlimited but a limited number of possible relations of elements. In Bénard convection cells, e.g., the liquid particles are offered the opportunity to engage in up-and-down moves where the move upwards, at a certain point in space and time, excludes the move downwards at the same point;

- The semantic aspect comes into play because inasmuch as it is energy input into the system that enables it to (re)structure its order, the input becomes a signal that gives rise to the new pattern, though not completely determining it. The signal makes the state the system adopts when forming the pattern a representation of the input. The state the system adopts 'means' for the system in question that the control parameter has exceeded a critical value beyond which it reacts, with a change from heat conduction to heat convection, whether or not the convection cells work clockwise, and;

- The pragmatic aspect comes up because pattern formation is tantamount to the behavior in which the system expresses its activity vis-à-vis the environment. The system changes its regime of heat transport through the liquid which is observable from the outside.

Though identifiable analytically, the semiosic aspects in systems on this stage of evolution are not yet unfolded; they are not yet differentiated from each other, they are one. The dynamic of these systems is characterized by only one process of self-organization. The result of this self-organization process is only one *signans*, one sign: the pattern (see Figure 11).

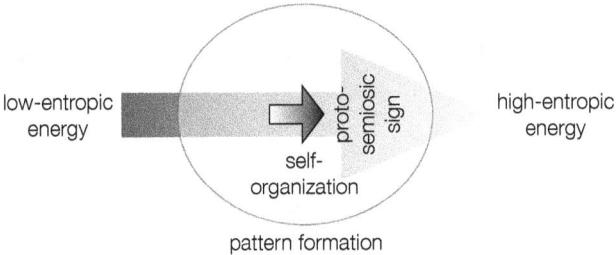

low-entropic energy   →   proto-semiosic sign   high-entropic energy

self-organization

pattern formation

Figure 11 *Pattern Formation as a One-Level Architecture of Self-Organization*

We can describe this stage of information generation as proto-semiosic or proto-syntactico-semanto-pragmatic.

It may be said that forming patterns is the way dissipative systems reflect (some change in the) conditions in the environment of the system. They have the ability to reflect. Simple self-organizing systems in the physical and chemical domains are instances of reflective systems. Yet evolution continues.

Q14. WHAT MAKES LIVING SYSTEMS CODE-MAKERS?

Codes are functional to narrow down (on the one hand) the possibilities of the self-organized build-up of order in living systems, and to give rise (on the other hand) to the realization of an abundancy of possibilities for survival. Codes regulate the decoding of signs that living systems produce when triggered by signals so as to reflect the affordance of objects/events for survival.

When the qualitative leap onto the stage of living-systems evolution occurred, physical and chemical systems refined the dissipation of entropy in that they exhibited the property of being able to maintain their order. They did this by organizing flows of energy and matter, by perpetuating the throughput of energy, by storing free energy, by producing the components that they were composed of, which made them turn from simple, dissipative to autopoietic, dissipative systems.

Living systems not only change their structure in a way which they choose themselves, within certain boundary conditions; they also introduce these changed structures into a broader context, namely in the context of how to let the structures contribute to maintaining their existence. Self-reproduction requires structures to be functionalized for survival. Functionalized structures are not plain patterns any more, but something that serves the function of survival. This is a distinction that cannot be attributed to the previous stage of evolutionary systems. Starting from the premise that autopoietic systems, that is, self-organizing systems in the biotic realm, are a sophistication of dissipative systems and evolved from self-organizing systems in the physical and chemical realm, we can identify another self-organization cycle that rests on top of the self-organization cycle already given, and 're-ontologizes' (a word I take from Luciano Floridi, 2007) the lower level. It's a two-level systems architecture that we are able to postulate here. Structures that serve functions appear. It is that which can be modelled by adding one level to the architecture of the systems (see Figure 12).

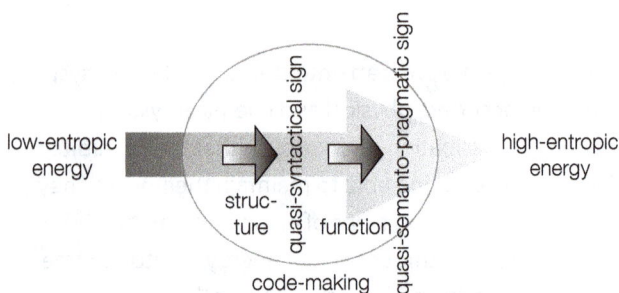

Figure 12 *Code-Making as a Two-Level Architecture of Self-Organization*

Based on these two self-organization cycles, the first on a structural level, and the second on a combined state/behavior level, we can distinguish between two information-generation processes.

Since living systems have an aim, they must be able to assess signals from the environment and assign significance to the objects these signals come from, according to the role these objects might play for the maintenance of their metabolism (Ayres, 1988 & 1994). It can be said that living systems show intended reactions on stimuli they take up. This is different from saying, as the old behavioristic dogma did, that there are strictly determined stimulus-response-relationships. There seems no way for prolonging the systems''life' and improving their adaptation to the environment, other than the establishment of another meta-level from which the first level can be interpreted in the light of survival necessities and survival possibilities.

As this interpretation is oriented towards a goal, as it is normative, there must be a rule that guides the interpretation. This rule can be denoted as code. Usually, a code is defined as a set of rules that establishes a correspondence between different sets of objects. So, sequences in DNA are said to correspond to protein sequences. This is also how Marcello Barbieri (2003) uses the term when referring to the ribotype as a code-maker that mediates between the genotype and the phenotype by decoding the genotype. However, we should be aware of the caveat that interpretation, at least basically, involves freedom of choice and that rules guide a process but never determine it or its results completely, unless the space of possibilities is restricted to only one possibility. Therefore, a code leaves enough room to move, though it channels the process into a certain direction. In the case of the genetic code this topic is known under the label of 'epigenesis'. The concept of code I am using here rather resembles the notions of cultural studies communication scientist Stuart Hall and of Luhmann than those used in a technical sense. Hall (1997) is known for replacing the Shannon-Weaver model of communication with one that emphasizes the contingency of the decoding process applied by human individuals. For Luhmann (1997), the code is that binary basic distinction on which a social system operates and by the application of what it observes. Both theories are true for living systems too. There is contingency in applying the code while decoding, on the one hand, because the code directs the interpretation towards survival and living systems cannot live without applying this code, on the other hand. So living systems are basically code-makers.

The tree of the evolution of semiosic relations hereby shows a ramification. The proto-semiosic, proto-syntactico-semanto-pragmatic line splits into a rather quasi-syntactical one and a quasi-semanto-pragmatic one.

Q15. IS THE CONSTITUTION OF SENSE IN HUMAN SYSTEMS DISTINCT FROM CODE-MAKING?

Social or human systems formed by, or represented by, humans are the instances of another stage of evolution of self-organizing systems and semiosis. Social systems are autopoietic systems which do not merely maintain themselves and strive for survival, but in doing so seek additional goals, which they are committed to and they have chosen on their own. While they aim at realizing these goals they aim at realizing themselves, and when they succeed they can be said to have created or re-created themselves; they are 're-creative' systems as Erich Jantsch characterized them (Jantsch, 1987; Holzkamp, 1983). They can create the conditions necessary not only for their reproduction, but also for creating themselves according to the goals they have set. They are free to restructure their environment, and with these alloplastic characteristics they are capable of restructuring themselves. As they alter their environment to suit what they themselves want to be, they exhibit even greater adaptability than non-human living systems. As a result of these characteristics, these systems exhibit a mature distinction between the state function and the output function (for behavior).

This means that another self-organization cycle is added on top of the two cycles characteristic of non-human living systems (see Figure 13). This new self-organization cycle reshapes the older two, so as to yield a new unity of diverse levels: these levels may be labelled as means, ways and goals, respectively (I owe these terms to the

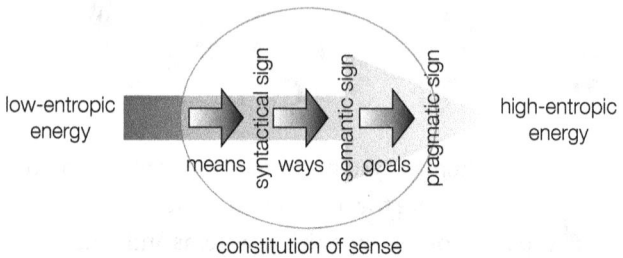

Figure 13 *Constitution of Sense as Three-Level Architecture of Self-Organization*

philosopher John Collier, in a personal communication), that is, if the hierarchical structure-function distinction is iterated by turning function 1 into structure 2 for another function 2, then structure 1 has to change too because it has to serve function 2 via function 1. Thus, the structure-function relationship is replaced by the means-ways-goals relationship.

This is consequential for the information generation processes too. Since social systems can be classified as self-producing this selection takes the shape of a decision which is made under the condition of an irreducible freedom of choice. Owing to the self-organization approach it is supposed that when they face a variety of behavioral options, which are possible under certain circumstances, it is up to the social systems to decide which option they select. This characterizes an emergent quality which makes the pragmatic distinct from the semantic. This difference becomes apparent when recognizing that, given a certain representation of a fact (which is 'mapped' by the state of the system in question), there will be a variety of normative guidelines for action compatible with it (which concern behavior). This is the well-known 'Is-Ought' problem.

Consequently, at the stage of social, re-creative, teleological, self-productive, systems another symmetry is broken, and the semiosic relations unfold into the well-known three levels of sign production, which together will be described here as the constitution of sense (in accordance with Luhmann, 1997. See Moeller, 2006: 225). 'Sense'—the German 'Sinn'—as different from 'meaning'—the German 'Bedeutung'—depicts something that re-ontologizes, reworks, restructures, the whole chain of lower levels from the goal, to the ways, to the means in social systems and is a term more concrete than the term 'meaning', which applies to each interpretation process and hence to information processes at any evolutionary stage of self-organizing systems.

The former quasi-semanto-pragmatic line branches into two distinct, but dependent, pragmatic and semantic lines, which together reshape the former quasi-syntactical line as syntactical.

Q16. HOW IS THE TRIPLE-C MODEL ENGAGED WITH EVOLUTIONARY SYSTEMS?

While the typology of evolutionary systems (dissipative, autopoietic, and re-creative systems) yields a typology of ever more sophisticated information generating processes (proto-semiosic, quasi-semiosic and semiosic information) along the course of evolution, it is the differentiation of different dimensions along the hierarchical build-up of systems that lays the foundations for the dimensions in which information processes occur: the cognitive, the communicative and the cooperative (Hofkirchner *et al.*, 2003).

Different system dimensions refer to different system phases or different system levels. The following phases are characteristic of the meta-system transition (Turchin *et al.*, 1999):

* In a first phase there is only a multitude of entities, which later on will become elements of the system to be formed. In this phase they cannot be addressed as elements because there is no system yet. They do not have bindings to each other at all. This phase may be called the pre-elementary phase, seen from the angle of the system to emerge;

* Only in the second phase do these entities begin to develop relations among themselves; they interact with each other. But this interactive relationship need not be durable or stable and can vanish according to the changing activities of the entities involved. In this

intermediate phase, processes may still be reversible, and;

- It is in a third phase that a system is formed during the course of interaction. Durable, stable relations are established among the entities which by then turn into elements of just this system. This integration phase makes the changes irreversible. A new system has emerged.

After the emergence of the meta-system three different levels remain which resemble historical transition and express a supra-system hierarchy:

- An intra-systemic level focusing exclusively on the internal processes of a system that is a constituent of the supra-system;

- An inter-systemic level focusing on the interrelations of these constituent systems, and;

- A supra-systemic level focusing on the supra-system that is 'external' to the constituents.

Now, information generation can be classified along these dimensions, characterized by phases and levels:

- What is going on in the (pre-)elementary phase respectively on the intra-systemic level in terms of information processes turns out as cognitive process. Cognition then is the individual, internal, generation of information (see Figure 14).

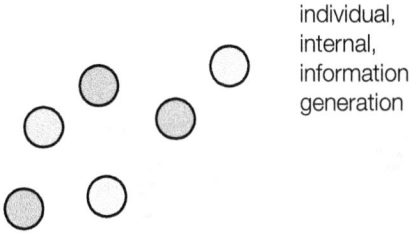

pre-elementary phase/
intra-systemic level:

individual,
internal,
information
generation

Figure 14 *Cognition Dimension*

- What is going on in the intermediate phase respectively on the inter-systemic level in terms of information processes is nothing other than communicative processes. Communication then is the interactional, interfacial, generation of information (see Figure 15).

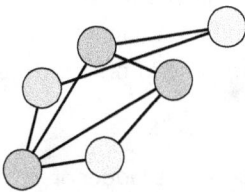

intermediate phase/
inter-systemic level:

interactional,
interfacial,
information
generation

Figure 15 *Communication Dimension*

- And what is going on in the integration phase respectively on the supra-systemic level in terms of information processes may be denoted as cooperative processes. Cooperation is then the collective, external, generation of information (see Figure 16).

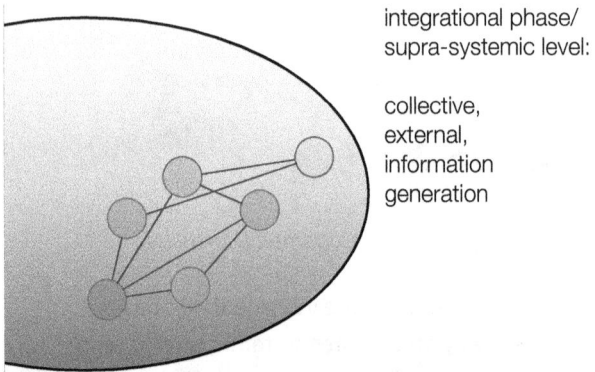

integrational phase/ supra-systemic level:

collective, external, information generation

Figure 16 *Cooperation Dimension*

Hierarchy always means that the higher level shapes the lower one, though the higher depends on the lower. That is to say, cognition is a necessary condition for communication, and communication is a necessary condition for cooperation, while, given a system of systems, cooperation of these very systems shapes their communication, which, in turn, shapes the cognition in each of them. In this way, cognition, communication and cooperation are mutually conditioned. This is the meaning of the Triple-C Model.

It is easy to see that we can iterate the ladder of complexity in both directions. What is cooperation at the higher end, turns into internal cognition of a supra-system. And what is cognition at the lower end, is a process and product of cooperation of subsystems.

It is important not to forget that 'cognition', 'communication' and 'cooperation' are not only meant for human systems but also for living systems and material systems, as long as they self-organize. We have to acknowledge cognizability, communicability and cooperability in non-human systems too.

This system theoretical assumption is backed by philosophical assumptions on the subject-object-relationship, by which we can elaborate on the semiotic considerations we have arrived at so far (Hofkirchner *et al.*, 2007).

There are different cases of the relationship between a subject and its object corresponding to the nature of the object:

- The object may be a simple one;
- It may be a co-subject, and;
- It may be a supra-subject.

A simple object is an object which is no subject at all (e.g. a mechanical system) or it is a subject of a simpler kind than that of the subject in question. A co-subject is a subject of the same kind, and a supra-subject is a subject of a more complex kind (usually one composed of co-subjects). According to these cases, we can differentiate between the accompanying information generation processes.

In the case of engaging with a simple object, we deal with the individual, internal generation of information in and by the subject. The opposing tendencies are subjection and objection tending toward an upward spiral in a three-step process (see Figure 17):

•   The subject acts on the object (subjection);

•   The object reacts (objection), and;

•   The subject changes its action by taking into account the reaction of the object to its past action (new subjection).

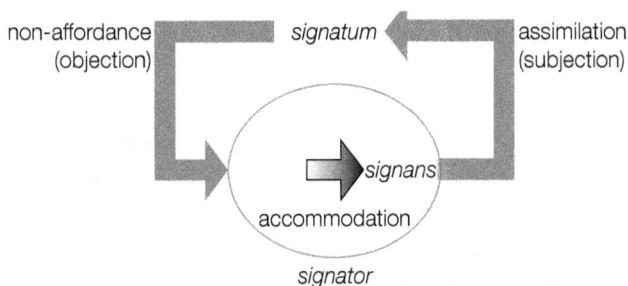

Figure 17 *Cognition*

Regarding information or sign generation, these steps involve assimiliation, non-affordance and accommodation (assimilation and accommodation being terms introduced by J. Piaget, 1976, 1980, and affordance being a term coined by J. J. Gibson, 1950, 1966, 1979). Assimilation is the informational or semiosic aspect of subjection. Affordance means the degree to which the object affords being subjected; non-affordance is the degree to which it does not. Finally, accommodation is what happens informationally or semiosically if the subject adapts to the object. Accommodation takes precedence over the next round of trying to subject the object. Thus intra-subjective information, that is, information in a cognitive sense, is created.

In the second case, not only cognition is involved. We are concerned with the interactional, interfacial generation of information in and by co-subjects. A number of (at least two) (co-)subjects interact. The opposing tendencies can be called countering inter-subjectification processes, which show the following steps (see Figure 18):

- Subject A acts on a subject B (inter-subjectification by A);

- Subject B reacts (inter-subjectification by B), and;

- Subject A changes its action by taking into account the reaction of subject B to its past action (new inter-subjectification by A).

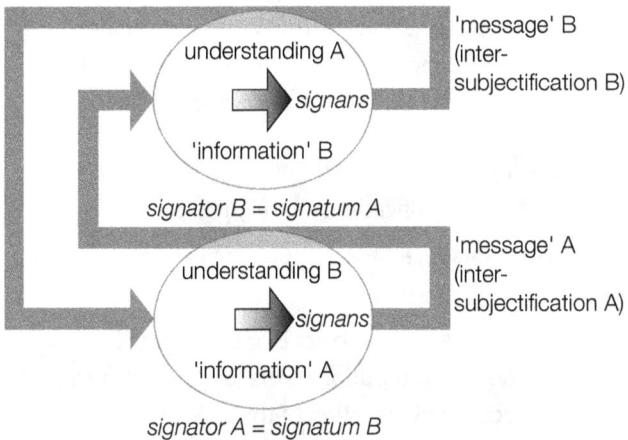

Figure 18 *Communication*

In informational or semiotic terms, in both subject A and subject B information generation or sign production is involved. Subject A bases its interaction with the other subject upon its being informed by this very subject, and so does subject B. That is, subject A starts the process with a given information. It reaches out to subject B and subject B informs itself about subject A's reaching out. This process can then be continued by subject B. Thus the inter-subjective information generation involves internal information generation with each of the sides. This ties up with the information-message-understanding distinction introduced by Luhmann (1997). Information in a communicative sense is created.

In the third case, it is not only communication that takes place. The focus is now on collective, external generation of information in which a critical number of co-subjects participate in the production of a common external. A *quorum* number of subjects co-act and the outcome of this very co-action is a supra-subject which, in turn, constrains and enables the co-subjects. The opposing tendencies may be called objectification and subjectification. The three steps of the spiralling-up process are as follows:

- Co-subjects A and B and C ... act conjointly on a supra-subject (objectification) (see Figure 19);
- The supra-subject reacts (subjectification) (see Figure 20), and;
- Co-subject A or co-subject B or co-subject C ... changes its contribution to the joint action by taking into account the reaction of the supra-subject to the past action of A or B or C ... (new objectification).

With regard to information generation and sign production, by communicating with each other co-subjects produce supra-subjective information which informs them in turn. That is, in a first perspective, by

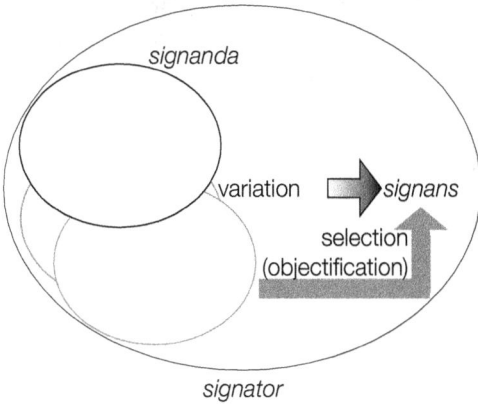

Figure 19 *Cooperation 1*

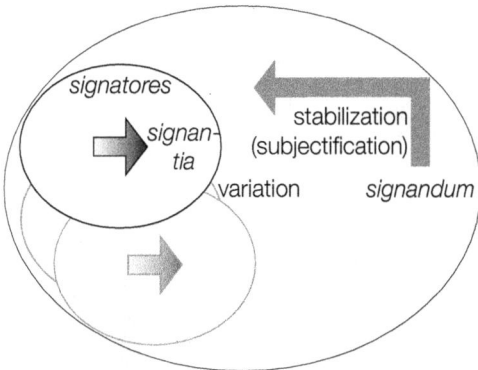

Figure 20 *Cooperation 2*

producing supra-subjective information they (re)produce
the supra-system as one sign-maker for which the sign
is functional and stands for the co-systems which are
so signified. In a second perspective, by reacting to the
supra-system, it instigates the co-systems as sign-makers
to (re)produce signs that stand for the supra-system
which is signifed (here we have got two perspectives; the
co-systems and the supra-system). This is in line with the

Luhman's categories of variation-selection-stabilization ('stabilization' is also called 'retention'; 1997). Information is created in a cooperative sense.

Q17. WHAT ARE THE PHYSICO-CHEMICAL ORIGINS OF COGNITION, COMMUNICATION AND COOPERATION?

We are now in a position to cross-table the information dimensions (triple-C—better: the cognition, communication, and cooperation abilities) with the information types (patterns, codes, sense—better: the abilities to form patterns, make codes, and constitute sense). The result is a 3-times-3 matrix of boxes covering the whole field of information categories. This is how a UTI can give a single picture of a multiplicity of information manifestations.

For reasons of better intuitive understanding, first, the dimensions are set as lines and the types as rows and, second, the order of the lines reflect the hierarchical architecture, in that line number 1 represents the uppermost level of cooperability and line number 3 represents the bottom level of cognizability, which is the ability to perform cognition processes.

For each line then we can see, jumping from row to row, a growing ability to recognize, to communicate and to cooperate. There are histories of unfolding cognizability, communicability and cooperability in evolutionary systems.

And for each row we have to keep in mind the self-organizing cascade that is typical of pattern-forming systems (one cycle only), code-making systems (two cycles) or sense-constituting systems (three cycles, eventually) and that has to be found at each of the triple-C levels.

In doing so, we can determine the categories of information generability (see Table 4).

Let's discuss the categories starting from systems that display the ability of pattern formation. From the cognitive point of view, pattern formation is a reflection of outside conditions (the change in the control parameter), like an echo. So 'reflectivity' is the notion that seems to suit this information category best; not in the sense of 'reflexivity' which is a capability said to be owned by human thinking only (as sociologist Margaret Archer, 2003, does) but in the sense of the German *Widerspiegelungsfähigkeit* which, as the philosophical writings of Lenin (who read Hegel) tried to insinuate, could and should be considered a fundamental property of all matter (Lenin, 1977: 53).

If a kind of echo is the cognitive aspect of primitive information generation, then the communicative aspect is a kind of resonance. Resonances demonstrate the

	pattern-formation ability	code-making ability	sense-con-stituting ability
cooperability	cohesiveness	organicity	sociability
communica-bility	coherency	signalability	languageability
cognizability	reflectivity	psyche	consciousness

Table 4 *Information Categories*

coherency between the sign(maker) and the signified as a result of the interaction.

On the cooperative side, what counts is cohesion, that is, emergent properties that hold a system together (see Collier, 1986; 1988; 2003), which is a collective effort and characteristic of each collectivity. So 'cohesiveness' might be the term we are looking for.

Q18. WHAT ARE THE PECULIARITIES OF BIO-COGNITION, BIO-COMMUNICATION AND BIO-COOPERATION?

Let's switch to the categories grasping the information generability of code-making systems.

As to the cognizability (the ability of cognition), I contend that there is no better choice than to name it 'psyche', which is the capability for flexible response. You might remember that 'flexible response' was the title of the NATO military doctrine valid during the Cold War, which meant officially that after a Soviet strike retaliation might or might not include nuclear bombing, or in other words, there should be no automatism in the NATO response that the Soviet Union could calculate, and many stages of the escalation ladder should be optional at any time at any location. Thus, in 1967, the Western military abandoned the stance of behaviorism in military affairs which, in the science of psychology, seemed to require much more effort to be overcome by understanding the psyche as an intermediary between stimuli and responses.

Cognition in the sense used here, comprises the universe of individual, internal information generation and is not restricted to one part of it, like the non-emotional or rational.

The two concatenated levels in cognition are sensitivity and motivatedness (see Figure 21).

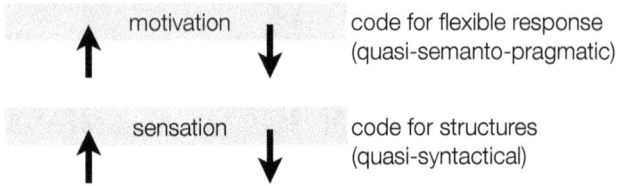

motivation → code for flexible response (quasi-semanto-pragmatic)

sensation → code for structures (quasi-syntactical)

Figure 21 *Layer Model of Bio-Cognition*

- Sensitivity refers to what are known as sensations in living systems. Sensations are self-organized restructurings which are evoked by perturbations, as Maturana and Varela like to term the signals from the outside, but are not strictly determined by them, and therefore not reducible to them. Sensational restructuring is constrained by the space of possible relationships that elements can enter into. This space of possibilities characterizes the potential of the sensorium and has a quasi-syntactical implication.

- Motivatedness refers then to the effectorium of living systems and to the process in which activities are endowed with motivations according to given sensations. Living systems act in response to what sensations mean. That is, they assign a meaning to the sensations and interpret them in terms of survival relevance. The sensational structures may mean that the stimulus they represent (which is the semantic part of the sign relation) is either beneficial or detrimental to the survival of the system or neutral (which is the pragmatic part of the sign relation). Sensations become a means to effectuation. The quasi-syntactical dimension of the new structure is supplemented by the fact that this difference makes a difference regarding the task of maintaining the system and the quasi-semanto-pragmatic dimension of codes is added.

By means of the sensation-motivation distinction, the possibility appears to decouple the response from the stimulus in living systems, to learn and usher in ever more intelligent systems. Yet, in contradistinction to human systems, representations and evaluations go hand in hand.

An example may be the recognition of predators. Whenever sensation is interpreted as an indication of, say, a snake or a raptor, the immediate (though context-dependent) proper activity will be motivated.

Bio-communication which is located at the interface of biosystems is made up of another two cycles:

• 'Re-presentation', and;
• Reorientation (see Figure 22).

'Re-presentations' is a term I borrow from Ernst von Glasersfeld (1995). He refers to Piaget and means that a child when recalling 're-presents', that is, 'presents again' the recalled to itself. I would like to use the term for describing the activity of presenting the cognition of one

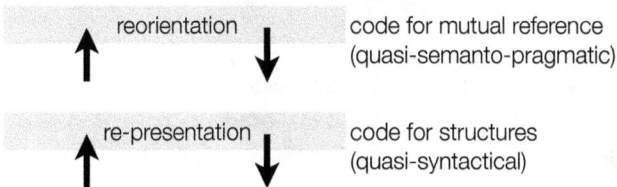

| reorientation | code for mutual reference (quasi-semanto-pragmatic) |
| re-presentation | code for structures (quasi-syntactical) |

Figure 22 *Layer Model of Bio-Communication*

biosystem to a co-biosystem, which may or may not lead to a reorientation in the experience of the second system which is, in turn, re-presented to the first system, and may or may not lead, in reciprocity, to a reorientation of the first system.

This communicability of biosystems may be called 'signalability'—the ability to make codes for mutual reference.

An example for signalability is the process of initiating the start of a resting flock of birds. According to some outer or inner conditions some of the birds give, mainly by movements of their wings, some indication of being motivated to fly which can be anticipated by their fellow birds, which then can react in their own way and either pass on the motive or show resistance to being infected, and may even succeed in calming down the original activists. It is clear that the ability of birds to interpret the behavior of other birds requires the ability to recognize.

Bio-cooperation, finally, concerns the division and bringing together of functions between co-systems (see Figure 23).

- On the one hand, there are specializations;
- But on the other, special structures have the function to complement each other for a common whole.

This ability to make codes for the division of functions may be called 'organicity', since it makes up the basic feature of organisms and organic order. The division of functions is a predecessor of the division of labour in social systems and

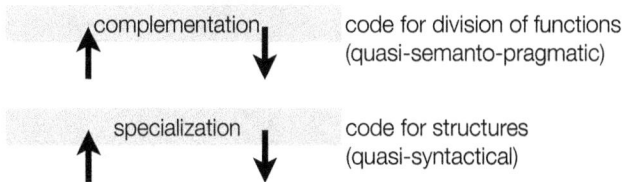

Figure 23 *Layer Model of Bio-Cooperation*

is true from the compartments of a single cell, through multi-cellular organisms, to the social organization of insects and vertebrates.

A well-known example is the eventual differentiation of originally independently living amoeba-like cells of *dictiostelium discoideum* when gathering to build a multi-cellular slime mould into cells, which form a stalk, and cells, which form spores (Hofkirchner *et al.*, 2007). It is clear that the ability to specialize requires the ability to communicate with other cells.

Organicity, signalability and psyche condition each other. Psychic abilities are the precondition for signalling abilities which, in turn, are the precondition for the ability to form an organic whole. Seen the other way round, an organic whole needs signalability between its parts, otherwise the division of functions would be made impossible. The parts each need psyche, otherwise the interpretation of signals between them would be made impossible.

Q19. WHAT ARE THE PECULIARITIES OF HUMAN COGNITION, COMMUNICATION AND COOPERATION?

Let's move now to the categories belonging to the field of systems capable of constituting sense.

Traditionally, in human cognition, the outstanding feature of human psyche is said to be consciousness, mind, reflexivity, self-consciousness, the ability to cry or laugh, empathy, creativity and so on. In human communication, it is the ability to speak, write and so on. And in human cooperation it is the ability for tool-making, tool-using, working, organizing, role-taking and so on. The problem we are facing is that whatever the feature might be it is contested by research results in animals and the border seems blurred. According to the methodology represented here, it is clear that the required notions have to be able to perform. Whatever notions are chosen, by those very notions something will be denoted that really distinguishes human psyche, signalability and organicity from prehuman psyche, signalability and organicity and, at the same time, has a general foundation in what human psyche, signalability and organicity, on the one hand, and prehuman psyche, signalability and organicity, on the other, have in common.

Now, what is common is that we find a distinction of levels in the information generating process. What is unique is that we find a tripartite distinction:

- In cognition, it is perception, interpretation and evaluation. Perception (which signifies the syntactical level) is made up of the opposing tendencies of receiving and conceiving. Interpretation (by which the semantic level is addressed) is a combination of an instructing process and a constructing process. And evaluation (which makes up the pragmatic level) is a feedback loop between describing and prescribing (see Figure 24). As a result of the difference of interpretation and evaluation, humans are capable of longing for wisdom, given knowledge. But things that do not make sense are possible too. This is part of the 'Is-Ought' Problem; norms cannot be concluded from facts, the semantic cognitive level is only the prerequisite of the pragmatic cognitive level.

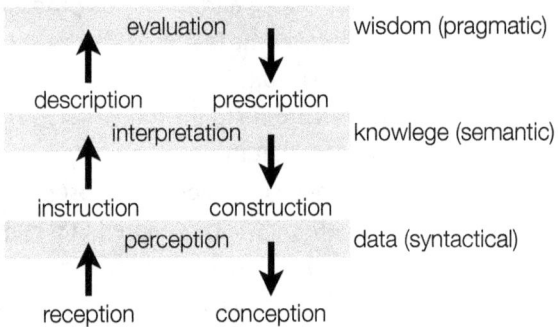

Figure 24 *Layer Model of Human Cognition*

- In communication, it is processes of tuning between *ego* and *alter* in the Luhmann's sense (1997) on the level of combinations of language particles (syntactical level), by which what is presented is expressed. This comprises the whole range of possible means of presenting one's cognition including non-verbal ones (expressive tuning), on the level of content (semantic level) which indicates what the cognitions that are exchanged are about (indicative tuning), as well as on the level of context (pragmatic level); that is, the relationship between *alter* and *ego*, the intention why *ego* wants to engage with *alter* and why he wants to appeal to her and vice versa, (appellative tuning). This is a tuning of expression, indication and appeal, on the one hand, and understanding, on the other, for *ego* and *alter* respectively (see Figure 25). It is a human feature that the meaning of a conversation only makes sense if the relationship of *alter* and *ego* and their intentions are considered (and then, sometimes, it might not make sense at all). This is languageability (a term originally introduced by Maturana and Varela).

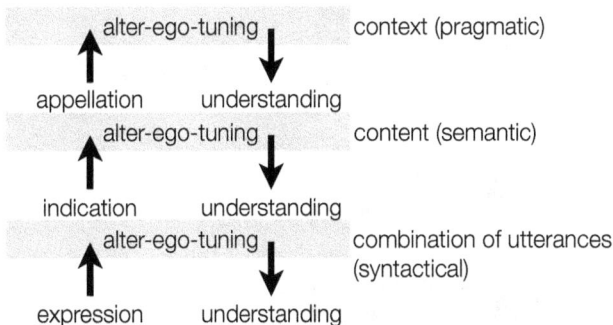

↑ alter-ego-tuning ↓	context (pragmatic)
appellation understanding	
↑ alter-ego-tuning ↓	content (semantic)
indication understanding	
↑ alter-ego-tuning ↓	combination of utterances (syntactical)
expression understanding	

Figure 25 *Layer Model of Human Communication*

• In cooperation, it is, first, a coordinated activity (to be located on a syntactical level) which uses and designs technologies as productive forces, and second, a collaborative work (to be identified on a semantic level), which uses and designs conditions of survival *(Umwelt)*. Third, it is a consensualized action (to be attached to the pragmatic level), which uses and designs sense which is the specific human cultural dimension of living a good life as Aristotle's *eudaimonia* denotes (see Figure 26). Sense is deemed to be transferred back and proliferate to the levels below, but a plethora of examples like climate change and enduring, bloody wars exemplify that there need not be sense at all. They demonstrate the reality of contradictory relationships between the levels and testify the uniqueness of the species *homo sapiens* on planet Earth, but at the same time the deficiencies of not yet being successful in emancipating humans from hereditary features that are detrimental to the persistence of humanity (hence *homo sapiens* is sometimes called *homo demens*). Anyway, this is human sociability.

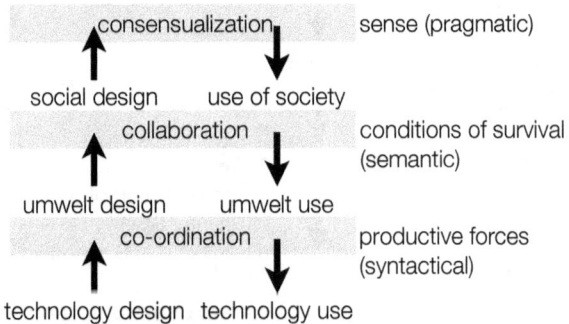

consensualization   sense (pragmatic)

social design   use of society
          collaboration   conditions of survival
                                (semantic)
umwelt design   umwelt use
          co-ordination   productive forces
                                (syntactical)
technology design   technology use

Figure 26 *Layer Model of Human Cooperation*

This particular distinction, the distinction between the second and the third levels, which bounces back to the first level, finds its origin in the transition from animal social life to human societal life.

There is a decisive leap in quality between socializing in the most advanced primates and sociability in humans. This new quality adds a new feature to evolution, which makes up a new level of semiosis.

Human cooperation is distinct from cooperation in the animal kingdom. In the animal kingdom, cooperation appears in the form of certain divisions of functions. So you can find the so-called 'aunt behavior' as a function in primates, or a kind of altruistic function in hoofed animals, which shows the self-sacrificing behavior of individual animals when the herd is chased by predators. Human cooperation takes on the form of a division of labour when at work, which serves as a model for different divided and composed actions and as a base for different roles that individuals play in the societal context. Human cooperation reveals insight into individual members in the societal context they form part of, as the famous hunter-beater example in Leontyev's activity theory demonstrates (Leontyev, 1981: 210-12). According to him, human actions are distinct from animal behavior in that they do not end in satisfying biotic needs but are mediated by a societal detour, and humans reflect this societal detour and are aware of it. They oversee (part of) the societal context and act accordingly. Actions make sense because of their embeddedness in commonly (societally) shared designs of activity relations, as a result of being part of a chain of actions, because of contributing to the maintenance of a whole system of interrelated actions.

If tools are involved in these actions, especially if they are devised and constructed for use and handed over to conspecifics and to their offspring, then these tools embody the meaning of the societal context and inherit the meaning of the societal context (Holzkamp, 1983). With the use or design of a tool its meaning is propagated. Not only is work and the division of labour the model for any action but it is also the meaning of the tools; the model for sense.

Human communication is fundamentally about expectations. What does *ego* expect from *alter*? What does *alter* expect *ego* to do? What does *alter* expect *ego* to expect from *alter*? Mutual expectations are formed in line with the sense that is constituted throughout the societal context.

Human cognition, in the form of thinking, reasoning and deliberating, originated from the crisis owing to the information overload that came along with the increase of complexity of our ancestors' social life when they acquired skills like tool-making, controlling fire, group foraging and coordinated hunting. Thinking is enabled to deal with that 'chaos' by creating concepts, that is, abstract ideas that result from the generalization of particular examples. In this regard, human cognition is distinct from animal cognition in that it is rather concept-based than percept-based (Logan, 2007). Human thinking enables humans to reflect themselves and to reflect themselves as part of a bigger picture, that is, society. Individual members of society can and do consider themselves as members of society, and they can and do consider other members as members. The social life of humans extends to the societal life. The actions of members towards other members of society is mediated by this third aspect: (the structure of) society. The reflection of this is a model for all (complex) thinking, that is, for grasping the general relationship between parts and whole, of which individual and society are just the model instantiation.

Taken together, we can visualize three evolutionary stage models of cognition, communication and cooperation.

Cognizability goes from patterns of reflection through codes for flexible response to sense of pro-action (see Figure 27).

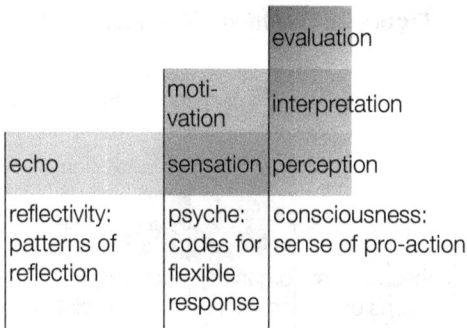

		evaluation
	moti-vation	interpretation
echo	sensation	perception
reflectivity: patterns of reflection	psyche: codes for flexible response	consciousness: sense of pro-action

Figure 27 *Evolution of Cognizability*

Communicability develops from patterns of coherence through codes for reference to sense of reciprocal action (see Figure 28).

And cooperability starts with patterns of cohesion, passes codes for division of functions and ends up at a sense of joint action (see Figure 29).

		appellative tuning
	reorien-tation	indicative tuning
resonance	re-pre-sentation	expressive tuning
coherency: patterns of coherence	signal-ability: codes for reference	languageability: sense of reciprocal action

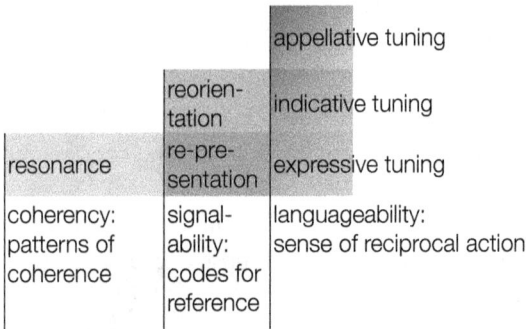

Figure 28 *Evolution of Communicability*

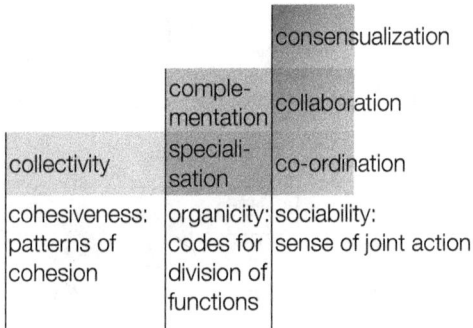

		consensualization
	comple-mentation	collaboration
collectivity	speciali-sation	co-ordination
cohesiveness: patterns of cohesion	organicity: codes for division of functions	sociability: sense of joint action

Figure 29 *Evolution of Cooperability*

Q20. WHY DO WE NEED COLLECTIVE INTELLIGENCE ON A PLANETARY SCALE?

Collective intelligence is the synergetic effect produced when intelligent agents cooperate; the intelligence produced when cooperation exceeds the intelligence of each of the agents.

From an evolutionary systems theory point of view, society is but another self-organizing system that constitutes that step in the overall evolution which represents the most sophisticated form of information generation. Over and above that, the issue can be raised as to whether this form of social information processing will, by means of electronic networking—that is, linking of humans and computers together—undergo a transformation to a new and higher level. That is to say, will a global brain not only be capable of monitoring the manifestations of crises in the socio-economic, environmental and technological spheres, but also enable humans to set world society on a path towards sustainable development, which is tantamount to a leap in societal self-organization?

Those who argue in favour of the thesis that the spread of computer-linked telecommunications will provide the hardware of an emerging global nervous system and brain, point out that after the inventions of speech, writing and the printing press, the diffusion of ICTs is setting the stage for extending human collective intelligence into novel socio-technical forms that might regain the inter-connectedness of bacteria (Bloom, 2000), if not transcend both the intelligence of humans and machines of today by even more than human information processing systems transcend pre-human ones (Haefner 1991). The introduction of each of the series of information technologies created closer and closer links between individuals and groups of individuals as elements and subsystems of social systems. So does the introduction of the electromagnetic communication technology and computerization. But they create interdependence at a planetary level. 'In principle, this process does not differ from the evolution of primitive nervous systems into advanced mammalian brains', says Tom Stonier (1992: 105):

Relatively few nerve cells, relatively poorly coordinated, evolving into an organ consisting of trillions of cells so exquisitely coordinated that our understanding of how it works still eludes us. With the evolution of the global brain we are dealing with a parallel process, but at a much higher level of complexity ... Each node, rather than being a neuron, is a person comprising trillions of neurons ... coupled ... to their personal computers ... We are now dealing with the very top end of the known spectrum of intelligence.

However, it is right to state that a change in quantity is only a necessary precondition, but not a sufficient one, for change in quality (Fleissner *et al.*, 1998). Interdependence is but a step towards integration, not integration itself. Like the qualitative leap dividing phenomena at the physiological level (that is, brain phenomena like electrical and chemical neuronal activity) from those at the psychological level (mind phenomena like states of consciousness and conscience), there is a jump required from the inter-connectivity of intelligent nodes in the global network, to the 'software' of something like a mind of global society.

Furthermore, the software to be run by the super-organism of a future world society, in order to be able to sense, interpret, and respond (Stock, 1993: 80-91), lacks reason, more than ever before. Societal development in this phase of transition is marked by sharp discrepancies: between the practice of technically unifying the world and the social theory of world unity; between the universe of communication of nation states, and the universal community of mankind (postulated time and again in models since the enlightenment); between the reality of globalization and the ideals of humanity, evolving a global mind including self-awareness, consciousness and conscience (Richter, 1992).

Today, existing societies lack the intelligence, logistics and organization which they need to secure their material reproduction, and to plan and carry out strategies which would set the world on a path towards sustainable development. Such development would go about solving problems such as the use of force for political means, the gap between rich and poor (both of nations and of individuals), and damage caused by pollution and the extraction of raw materials. This obvious capacity for self-destruction is a sign that the global development of society has entered a decisive phase; a phase in which the degree of complexification and differentiation reached can be compensated for by the opposite trend of simplification and integration into a newly-created supra-system. Contrary to evolutionary information-processing systems on the pre-human level, the kind of self-organization which is needed to overcome the crises in question requires actions of conscious individuals, and will not emerge from technological progress alone (Laszlo, 1989).

Seen from this point of view, the idea of a global brain becomes functional when viewed in the context of a possible transformation of the evolution of consciousness into conscious evolution (see Figure 30). Béla H. Banathy, the advocate of social systems design, takes as his point of departure a quotation of Jonathan Salk (1983: 112): '... human beings now play an active and critical role not only in the process of their own evolution but in the survival and evolution of all things.' As Banathy (2003: 203) adds:

> *If we accept this responsibility and engage creatively in the work of evolution we shall ... be the designers of our future, we shall become the guides of our own evolution and the evolution of life on earth and possibly beyond.*

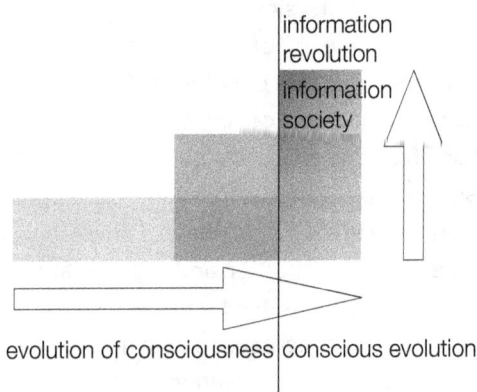

Figure 30 *From Evolution of Consciousness to Conscious Evolution*

This becomes crucial, in particular, because society has to be empowered to cope with global challenges in several respects. Society has to be endowed with a means to enhance its problem-solving capacity regarding the challenges it is confronted with. Society has to be enabled to meet the growing demand for governance in the face of tendencies of fragmentation, heterogenization and disintegration.

According to Western thinking, since the days of Francis Bacon the role science and technology have been thought to play in society may have been for a better life. But now that the apparent effects have come to jeopardize the aims in pursuit of which inventions and innovations were originally carried out to such an extent that civilization is at stake, the programme of Bacon must be overhauled in the light of Bacon's ideals, and rationality criticized from the angle of reason. In this situation, reshaping science and technology is a task whose time has come.

Given that it is a shared value to improve, or at least to maintain, living conditions for the human race on this planet, the purpose of scientific and technological efforts is to provide a means of coping with global problems. What is needed is self-reflection in scientific and technological progress; that is, the application of scientific endeavour to scientific endeavour itself, in order to redirect scientific-technological progress and to help overcome the fundamental failures of modernity, the application of research and development methods to science and technology for the purpose of their own control. Science and technology can do justice to their original purpose—to alleviate human life and generally make that life more pleasant—only when they are no longer left to pursue their seemingly natural course. Instead of being left to their own dynamics, they should be put into operation deliberately, after appropriate reflection and careful consideration, and should be managed with conscious control, that is, when their programme is executed with respect to the ideals of the survival of humanity in a future which is worth living in, and when a constant control of the results of the implementation of the programme is instituted. That means that science must devote careful consideration to its technological consequences in society, must anticipate possible desired or undesired effects, and must carry out any appropriate readjustments or reorientations.

Science and technology in that sense are part and parcel of the global brain for a global sustainable information society to come, as global consciousness is.

A UTI may contribute to the required self-reflection of science and technology.

REFERENCES

Archer, M. (2007). *Making our Way through the World, Human Reflexivity and Social Mobility,* ISBN13 9780521696937.

Atmanspacher, H., Kurths, J., Scheingraber, H., Wackerbauer, R. and Witt, A. (1992). "Complexity and meaning in nonlinear dynamical systems," *Open Systems and Inf. Dynamics,* ISSN 1230-1612, 2(1): 269-289.

Atmanspacher, H. and Scheingraber, H. (1990). "Pragmatic information and dynamical instabilities in a multimode continuous-wave dye laser," *Can. J. Phys.,* ISSN 0008-4204, 68: 728-737.

Ayres, R.U. (1988). "Self-organization in biology and economics," *Int. J. Unity of the Sc.,* ISSN 0896-2294, 3(1): 267-304.

Ayres, R.U. (1994). *Information, Entropy, and Progress,* ISBN 0883189119.

Banathy, B.H. (2000). *Guided Evolution of Society. A Systems View,* ISBN13 9780306463822.

Barbieri, M. (2003). *The Organic Codes: An Introduction to Semantic Biology,* ISBN 0521824141.

Bateson, G. (1972). *Steps to an Ecology of Mind,* ISBN 0700201807.

Bishop, R.C. (2008). "Downward causation in fluid convection," *Synthese,* DOI 10.1007/s11229-006-9112-2, 160: 229-248.

(no author, no date). "Blind Men and an Elephant," http://en.wikipedia.org/wiki/Blind_Men_and_an_Elephant

Blitz, D. (1992). *Emergent Evolution: Qualitative Novelty and the Levels of Reality,* ISBN 0792316584.

Bloom, H. (2000). *The Global Brain: The Evolution of Mass Mind From the Big Bang to the 21st Century,* ISBN 0471295841.

Brier, S. (2008). *Cybersemiotics: Why Information Is Not Enough,* ISBN13 9780802092205.

Brier, S. (1999). "Biosemiotics and the foundation of cybersemiotics," *Semiotica,* ISSN 0037-1998, 127(1/4): 169-198.

Brockman, J. (1995). *The Third Culture, Beyond the Scientific Revolution,* ISBN 0684803593.

Brunner, K. and Klauninger, B. (2003). "An integrative image of causality and emergence", in V. Arshinov and C. Fuchs (eds.), *Emergence, Causality, Self-Organization,* ISBN 5956200065, pp. 23-35.

Bunge, M. (1980). *The Mind-Body Problem,* 0080247202.

Capurro, R. (1978). *Information,* ISBN 3598070896.

Capurro, R., Fleissner, P. and Hofkirchner, W. (1997). "Is a unified theory of information feasible?", *World Futures*, ISSN 0260-4027, 3-4(49) & 1-4(50): 213–234.

Capurro, R. and Hjørland, B. (2003). "The concept of information," *ARIST*, ISSN 0066-4200, 37: 343-411.

Collier, J. (2003). "Hierarchical dynamical information systems with a focus on biology", *Entropy*, ISSN 1099-4300, 5: 57-78.

Collier, J. (1988). "Supervenience and reduction in biological hierarchies," in M. Matthen and B. Linsky (eds.), *Philosophy and Biology*, ISBN 0919491146, pp. 209-234.

Collier, J. (1986). "Entropy in evolution," *Biology and Philosophy*, 0169- 3867, 1: 5-24.

Coulter, N.A.J. and Johnson, A.L. (1982). "Teleogenic systems theory as a metasystem methodology", Paper presented at the General Survey of Systems Methodology, Proceedings of the 26th Annual Meeting of the Society for General Systems Research, Louisville KY, USA.

Coveney, P., and Highfield, R. (1990). *The Arrow of Time*, ISBN 1852271973.

Emmeche, C. (1998). "Defining life as a semiotic phenomenon," *Cybernetics and Human Knowing*, ISSN 0907-0877, 5(1): 3–17.

Fenzl, N. and Hofkirchner, W. (1997). "Information processing in evolutionary systems. An outline conceptual framework for a unified information theory," in F. Schweitzer (ed.), *Self-Organization of Complex Structures: From Individual to Collective Dynamics,* Foreword by Hermann Haken, ISBN 9056990276, pp. 59-70.

Fleissner, P. and Hofkirchner, W. (1998). "The making of the information society: driving forces, 'leitbilder' and the imperative for survival," *BioSystems,* ISSN 1537-5110, 46: 201-207.

Fleissner, P. and Hofkirchner, W. (1997). "Actio non est reactio: an extension of the concept of causality towards phenomena of information," *World Futures,* ISSN 0260-4027, 3–4(49) & 1–4(50)/1997, 409–427.

Floridi, L. (2007). "A look into the future impact of ICT on our lives," *The Information Society,* ISSN 0197-2243, 23(1): 59-64.

Floridi, L. (2004). "Information," in L. Floridi (ed.), *The Blackwell Guide to the Philosophy of Computing and Information,* ISBN13 9780631229186, pp. 40-61.

Gerthsen, C., Kneser, H. O. and Vogel, H. (1995). *Physik,* ISBN 0387566384.

Gibbons, M. and Nowotny, H. (2002). "The potential of transdisciplinarity," in J. Thompson Klein et al. (eds.), *Transdisciplinarity: Joint Problem Solving among Science, Technology, and Society, An Effective Way for Managing Complexity,* ISBN 3764362480, pp. 67-80.

Gibson, J.J. (1979). *The Ecological Approach to Visual Perception,* 089859958X.

Gibson, J.J. (1966). *The Senses Considered as Perceptual Systems,* Boston: Houghton Mifflin.

Gibson, J.J. (1950). *The Perception of the Visual World,* Boston: Houghton Mifflin.

Goerner, S.J. (1994). *Chaos and the Evolving Ecological Universe,* ISBN 2881246354.

Haefner, K. (1991). *The Evolution of Information Processing Systems,* ISBN 3540550232.

Haken, H. (1988). *Information and Self-Organization,* ISBN 0387186395.

Hall, S. (1997). "Encoding and decoding," in P. Marris (ed.), *Media Studies,* ISBN 0748612068, pp. 41-49.

Hausman, C. (1993). *Charles S. Peirce's Evolutionary Philosophy,* ISBN 0521415594.

Heuser-Keßler, M.-L. (1992). *Schelling's Concept Of Self-Organization,* Berlin: Springer.

Heylighen, F. (2008). "Accelerating socio-technological evolution: From ephemeralization and stigmergy to the global brain," in G. Modelski, T. Devezas and W. Thompson (eds.), *Globalization as an Evolutionary Process: Modeling Global Change,* ISBN13 9780415773614, pp. 284-309.

Heylighen, F. (1990). "Autonomy and cognition as the maintenance and processing of distinctions," in F. Heylighen, E. Rosseel, and F. Demeyere (eds.), *Self-Steering and Cognition in Complex Systems, Toward a New Cybernetics*, ISBN 2881247296, pp. 89-106.

Hoffmeyer, J. (1996). *Signs of Meaning in the Universe*, ISBN 0253332338.

Hofkirchner, W. (2009). "A unified theory of information. An outline," http://bitrumagora.files.wordpress.com/2010/02/uti-hofkirchner.pdf.

Hofkirchner, W. (2007). "A critical social systems view of the internet," *Philosophy of the Social Sciences*, ISSN 0048-3931, 37(4): 471-500.

Hofkirchner, W. (2004). "Unity through diversity: Dialectics – systems thinking – semiotics," *Trans*, ISSN 1560-182X, 15: http://www.inst.at/trans/15Nr/01_2/hofkirchner15.htm.

Hofkirchner, W. (2002). *Projekt Eine Welt: Kognition – Kommunikation – Kooperation. Versuch über die Selbstorganisation der Informationsgesellschaft*, ISBN 3825860256.

Hofkirchner, W. (1998). "Emergence and the logic of explanation: An argument for the unity of science," *Acta Polytechnica Scandinavica*, Mathematics, Computing and Management in Engineering Series, ISSN 0001-6861, 91: 23–30.

Hofkirchner, W. (ed.) (1999). *The Quest for a Unified Theory of Information: Proceedings of the Second Conference on the Foundations of Information Science,* ISBN 905700531X.

Hofkirchner, W. and Ellersdorfer, G. (2007). "Biological information: Sign processes in living systems," in M. Barbieri (ed.), *Biosemiotic Research Trends,* ISBN13 9781600215742, pp. 141-155.

Hofkirchner, W., Fuchs, C. and Klauninger, B. (2005). "Informational universe: A praxeo-onto-epistemological approach," in E. Martikainen (ed.), *Human Approaches to the Universe, Interdisciplinary Studies,* ISBN 9519047948, pp. 75-94.

Hofkirchner, W. and Stockinger, G. (2003). "Towards a unified theory of information," *404nOtF0und,* ISSN 1676-2916, 1/24 (January): http://www.facom.ufba.br/ciberpesquisa/404nOtF0und/404_24.htm.

Holz, H.H. (1992). *Gottfried Wilhelm Leibniz,* ISBN 3593346303.

Holzkamp, K. (1983). *Grundlegung der Psychologie,* ISBN 3593331799.

Jantsch, E. (1987). "Erkenntnistheoretische aspekte der selbstorganisation natürlicher systeme," in S.J. Schmidt (ed.), *Der Diskurs des Radikalen Konstruktivismus,* ISBN 3518282360, pp. 159-191.

Kanitscheider, B. (1993). *Von Der Mechanistischen Welt Zum Kreativen Universum,* ISBN 3534112962.

Küppers, B.-O. (2000). "Die Strukturwissenschaften als Bindeglied zwischen Natur- und Geisteswissenschaften," in B.-O. Küppers (ed.), *Die Einheit der Wirklichkeit*, ISBN 3770534212, pp. 89-105.

Laszlo, E. (1989). *Global Denken*, ISBN 3926116110

Lenin, W. I. (1977). *Materialismus und Empiriokritizismus*, Berlin: Dietz.

Leontyev, A. N. (1981). *Problems of the Development of the Mind*, Moscow: Progress.

Lighthill, J. (1986). "The recently recognized failure of predictability in Newtonian dynamics," *Proc. R. Soc.*, ISSN 0950-1207, A 407: 38.

Logan, R. (2007). *The Extended Mind, The Emergence of Language, the Human Mind and Culture*, ISBN13 9780802093035.

Luhmann, N. (1997). *Die Gesellschaft der Gesellschaft*, ISBN 3518582402.

Mainzer, K. (1994). *Thinking in Complexity: The Complex Dynamics of Matter, Mind, and Mankind*, ISBN 3540575979.

Maturana, H. R. and Varela, F. (1980). *Autopoeisis and Cognition*, ISBN 9027710155.

Mayr, E. (1974). "Teleological and teleonomic: A new analysis," *Boston Studies in the Philosophy of Science*, ISSN 0068-0346, XIV: 91-117.

Moeller, H.-G. (2006). *Luhmann Explained: From Souls to Systems,* ISBN 978-0812695984.

Morin, E. (1999). *Seven Complex Lessons in Education for the Future,* ISBN 9231037781.

Nöth, W. (2000). *Handbuch der Semiotik,* ISBN 3476012263.

Piaget, J. (1980). *Abriß der genetischen Epistemologie,* ISBN 3129363408.

Piaget, J. (1976). *Die Äquilibration der kognitiven Strukturen,* ISBN 3129265309.

Peirce, C. S. (1983). *Phänomen und Logik der Zeichen,* ISBN 3518280252.

Peirce, C. S. (2000). *Semiotische Schriften,* ISBN 3518065882.

Popper, K. (1966). *Of Clouds and Clocks: An Approach to the Problem of Rationality and the Freedom of Man—The Arthur Holly Compton Memorial Lecture,* Washington: Washington University.

Popper, K.R. and Eccles, J.C. (1977). *The Self and Its Brain,* ISBN 0387083073.

Prigogine, I. (1980). *From Being to Becoming,* ISBN 0716711079.

Richter, E. (1992). *Der Zerfall de Welteinheit. Vernunft und Globalisierung in der Moderne,* ISBN 3593346613.

Salk, J. (1983). *Anatomy of Reality: Merging of Intuition and Reason,* ISBN 0231053282.

Seife, C. (2007). *Decoding the Universe. How the New Science of Information is Explaining Everything in the Cosmos, From Our Brains to Black Holes,* ISBN13 9780143038399.

Shannon, C. E. (1948). "A mathematical theory of communication," *The Bell System Technical Journal,* ISBN 0005-8580, 27(July, October): 379-423, 623-656.

Snow, C. P. (1998). *The Two Cultures: A Second Look,* ISBN 052109576X.

Stock, G. (1993). *Metaman: The Merging of Humans and Machines into a Global Superorganism,* ISBN 067170723X.

Stokes, D. (1997). *Pasteur's Quadrant: Basic Science and Technological Innovation,* ISBN 0815781784.

Stonier, T. (1992). *Beyond Information: The Natural History of Intelligence,* ISBN 0387196544.

Taborsky, E. (2001). "The internal and the external semiosic properties of reality," *SEED,* ISSN 1492-3157, 1(1).

Turchin, V. and Joslyn, C. (1999). "The metasystem transition," http://pespmc1.vub.ac.be/MSI.html

von Glasersfeld, E. (1995). *Radical Constructivism,* ISBN 0750703873.

von Foerster, H. (1960). "On self-organizing systems and their environments," in H. von Foerster (ed.), *Cybernetics of Cybernetics,* Minneapolis: Future Systems, pp. 220-230.

von Foerster, H. and Zopf, G.W. (eds.) (1962). *Principles of Self-Organization,* Oxford: Pergamon Press.

Weingartner, P. (1996). "Müssen wir unseren Gesetzesbegriff revidieren?", in P. Weingartner (ed.), *Gesetz und Vorhersage,* ISBN 3495478329, pp. 179-222.

Wilson, E.O. (1998). *Consilience: The Unity of Knowledge,* ISBN 0316645699.

Windelband, W. (1894). "Geschichte und Naturwissenschaft. Rede zum Antritt des Rektorats der Kaiser-Wilhelms-Universität-Straßburg, gehalten am 1. Mai 1894," http://www.fh-augsburg.de/~harsch/germanica/Chronologie/19Jh/Windelband/win_rede.html

ABOUT THE AUTHOR

Wolfgang Hofkirchner was born in 1953 in Vienna, Austria. Being educated as Political Scientist and Psychologist, he has been working since in the field of Science–Technology–Society. He has performed research and teaching at the Austrian Academy of Sciences; the Vienna University of Technology; the Federal University of Bahía, Salvador, Brazil; the Paris-Lodron University of Salzburg, Austria; the University of León, Spain; and the Open University of Catalonia, Barcelona. He founded the Unified Theory of Information Research Group, the open-access online journal for a Global Sustainable Information Society, triple-C, is director of the Bertalanffy Center for the Study of Systems Science, and member of the board of directors of the Science of Information Institute, Washington. His current focus is on an integrative science of information, information society and information technology. The perspective taken is that of complexity thinking underpinned by considerations rooted in philosophy while extending to ICTs and society.

http://www.hofkirchner.uti.at/